Death Railway

Clifford Kinvig

BB

Editor-in-Chief: Barrie Pitt
Editor: David Mason
Art Director: Sarah Kingham
Picture Editor: Robert Hunt
Consultant Art Editor: Denis Piper
Designer: David Allen
Illustration: John Batchelor
Photographic Research: Jonathan Moore
Cartographer: Richard Natkiel

Photographs for this book were especially selected from the following archives: from left to right pages 2–3 Australian War Memorial, Canberra; 8 Fujifotos, Tokyo; 10 US Army, Washington; 10–11 Keystone Press Agency, Tokyo; 12–17 Fujifotos; Keystone; 20–21 US Air Force, Washington; 23 Alexander Turnbull Library, New Zealand; 23–27 Fujifotos; 28–29 AWM; 30 Turnbull Library; 31 US National Archives, Washington; 31 AWM; 32–33 Turnbull Library; 34–47 GS Gimson, Edinburgh; 48 Shigeo Fujii, Tokyo; 51 AWM; 52–56 Gimson; 57 Fox Photos, London; 60–61 AWM; 62–63 Gimson; 64 AWM; 66–68 Gimson; 70–71 AWM; 72–73 National Archives; 74 Imperial War Museum, London; 75 Keystone; 76 IWM; 77 USAF; 77 IWM; 77 USAF; 80 Shigeo Fujii; 81 Radio Times–Hulton Picture Library, London; 82 Fujifotos; 84–93 Gimson; 95 IWM; 96–101 Gimson; 104 AWM; 107 Gimson; 108–109 Keystone; 110–111 Gimson; 112–115 Auckland Collection, St Albans; 118–121 Gimson; 122–123 AWM; 125 IWM; 126–127 National Archives; 128–134 IWM; 135 AWM; 136–139 IWM; 140 National Archives; 141 Fox; 142–143 National Archives; 144–145 US Army; 146–149 Turnbull Library; 150 US Army; 151–153 AWM; 154–155 Gimson; 156–157 AWM.
Front and back cover G S Gimson.
The publishers wish to extend special thanks to Mr G S Gimson of Edinburgh, Scotland for his permission to reproduce his drawings in this book.

Ballantine Books Inc.
101 Fifth Avenue New York NY10003

An Intext Publisher

with the enemy on a project vital to him: and when very few others in the Western world understand either Japan's wartime strategy or her code of military honour?

Until now this has been a question we Westerners have not only failed to answer: it is a question we have scrupulously avoided asking. Now, however, Major Kinvig has asked himself the question: and has answered it brilliantly. So brilliantly that no one, ex-captive or non-captive, impressed Asian or liberated Asian, Japanese soldier or Japanese civilian, can be anything but grateful to him. For here is the perfect mosaic.

In it are all our camps and cuttings and corpses; all our despair; all of Western civilization's ill-informed revulsion and Japan's implacable code of honour. In it is presented the case for the building of such a railway, and an evocation of the tragedy of it. Here at last all our subjective memories are set with compassion among the facts of history to provide the truth, part of which is that the Japanese, who won such brilliant victories in early 1942 that the Thailand Railway became an inevitability, were a formidable race. They remain formidable.

Until the last moment not a single Japanese soldier allowed himself to contemplate defeat. And though the Emperor called a halt to the war on 15th August 1945, Japan has gone on to win the peace with precisely that frenzy of energy, zeal and patriotism that enabled a handful of her engineers and ordinary soldiers to drive *us* to drive a railway, in an incredibly short time, straight through the malaria – infested gut of Thailand. Here surely there is a lesson about them to be learned?

Not that it is a lesson they have avoided trying to teach us in the past. Saipan should have taught us: where not only Japanese soldiers died to a man, rather than surrender, but women and children as well. Nowra should have taught us: Nowra, in New South Wales, Australia, from whose prisoner-of-war compound hundreds of Japanese, captured unconscious in the jungles of New Guinea, sought death by a breakout rather than risk the dishonour of eventual repatriation.

Kamikazes should have taught us; Okinawa should have taught us; Toshikasu Kasé should have taught us. Toshikasu Kasé who, as long ago as 1949, wrote a book called *The Eclipse of the Rising Sun;* and in that book ascribed Japan's eclipse not to the Americans or the British or the Dutch or the Australians–but to the Chinese, against whom, quite unavailingly, his country had fought so long. Toshikasu Kasé warned that it must not happen again. Major Kinvig warns that a race that could make a Thailand Railway necessary, and then build it, is a race quite different from any Western race.

Defending an Empire

In May 1942 the monsoon broke over Burma, quickly swelling the great Irrawaddy and Chindwin rivers, turning dried-up watercourses into raging torrents and rapidly transforming every dirt track which passed for a road in this forgotten corner of Empire into a morass of mud and silt. Soaked to the skin, the weary soldiers of the defeated Burma Corps struggled across the Chindwin river and up the tracks to the Imphal Plain, the great plateau ringed by the hills of northeast Assam which was henceforth to be the outpost of what was left of Allied power in South East Asia. With the coming of the rains, the dust began to settle after the awesome explosion of military power with which the Japanese Empire had opened the Pacific War. In Burma the Japanese offensive finally expended itself at the banks of the Chindwin river, where the Imperial soldiers, exhausted and with over-stretched supply lines, halted after harrying the British rearguards for over 1,000 miles, during the longest retreat in British military history. While General Slim's corps had retreated north westwards to the welcome but inhospitable sanctuary of the Imphal Plain, their allies in the battle for Burma, the Chinese forces of US General 'Vinegar Joe' Stilwell, had been pushed across the Salween river into Yunnan. China was now totally isolated; its last remaining land lifeline, the Burma Road, which ran from Rangoon, the capital of Burma, up to Chungking in the high Yunnan mountains, was in Japanese hands.

This story of Japanese victory in Burma was matched by equally rapid conquests across a great swathe of Asian and Pacific territory extending down through Indo-China and the Malayan Peninsula to the countless scattered islands of the Dutch East Indies and the Philippines, and on beyond them to wild New Guinea,

Japanese mountain guns are carried into the Burma hills

moon-shaped New Britain, the stepping-stone Solomons, the tiny Gilbert Islands and finally northwards across an expanse of ocean to the desolate islands of Attu and Kiska in the Aleutian chain. These conquests Japan added to those other territories she had amassed in 1895 during her wars against the Manchu dynasty in China, in 1905 against Imperial Russia and at the peace conference which parcelled out the Pacific territories of the beaten Germany in 1919. However, Japan's biggest holding on the Asian mainland was Manchuria, which she had transformed into the puppet state of Manchukuo, and adjacent to it a belt of eastern China in places 300 miles wide, stretching from the coast to the upper reaches of the Yellow River. Indeed it was Japan's war with China, or as the Japanese preferred to call it 'the settlement of the Peking incident,' which had forced her into the Pacific War against much more redoubtable adversaries than Chiang Kai-shek's Kuomintang divisions. The United States had looked with an increasing concern that finally turned to anger, at the depradations of the Japanese military on mainland China, but America's early efforts at persuading Japan to end her war of conquest had met only with evasion and prevarication. Finally, in 1940, the United States decided to employ the tool of diplomacy which she had hitherto been loath to use, namely the imposition of economic sanctions to force Japan to end the China War. It was a decision which America's allies were encouraged to support. In September she stopped the export of iron and steel to Japan and the Dutch authorities turned down the Japanese request for a long-term oil contract. In the summer of 1941 the pressure was increased; Britain placed an embargo on rubber exports from Malaya, and finally the United States imposed the crucial sanction: the export of oil to Japan was forbidden and all Japanese assets in the United States were frozen.

Above: Lieutenant-General Stilwell, commander of the Chinese forces in Burma. *Right:* Japanese troops on the China front

These belated actions made the Pacific War inevitable. Japan's war with China had started in 1931 in a limited way with the invasion of Manchuria, and it had developed into a full-scale conflict after the so-called 'Peking Incident' of 1937, after which the military forces had pushed deeper and deeper into Chinese territory; but to bring the war to a successful conclusion the Japanese needed more supplies, more weapons and more vehicles. To halt the China conflict short of victory was unthinkable to the commanders in the field and scarcely less so to the military leaders who now constituted the effective government of metropolitan Japan. But the alternative of expanding the war in order to produce a decision was now ruled out by the action of the Western powers, for without the imports of iron and oil Japan's war industries were hamstrung. The only solution therefore was for Japan to take by force the raw materials which she could not

Japanese troops advance through rubber plantations in Malaya

provide herself but which were so vital to the prosecution of the China War. These raw materials lay in the Asian outposts of the European Empires; in the Dutch East Indies, Borneo, Malaya, Burma and the Philippines. These territories grew the rice which could feed Japan's rapidly expanding population, the minerals, chemicals and the rubber which could sustain her war in Asia, and the oil which was the lifeblood of her economic system. In the evolving Japanese war plan these vital territories were termed the 'Southern Resources Area.'

The end of 1941 seemed the ideal time to strike; Holland had been overrun with consummate ease by Japan's ally, Germany; Britain was an embattled island fighting for her own life and the defence of her Middle East base, while France lay under the hand of the Axis powers and her Vichy government was weak and compliant. Most important of all, the Soviet Union – the traditional enemy of Japan – was now engaged in a life-and-death struggle with Germany, whose *blitzkrieg* forces were expected to have penetrated to the Soviet capital by December. With her northern frontier thus secure, Japan resolved to strike southwards at the end of the year if her negotiations with the United States, apparently as isolationist as ever, had not brought the concessions she required.

These apparently compelling strategic considerations were backed by a social, political and economic argument in which many educated Japanese sincerely believed; namely that Japan, by pushing the European imperial armies out of South East Asia and the Pacific, would be creating what was magnificently titled 'The Greater East Asia Co-prosperity Sphere', in which the various regions invaded by Japan would be liberated from the exploitation of the white man, and brought to affluence under Japanese guidance. This policy of 'Asia for the Asians' made an im-

mediate appeal to some of the embryonic nationalist movements in South East Asia. For many Japanese statesmen who were otherwise unwilling to see their country pushed into the Pacific War, the realisation of this dream of liberation provided the sole justification for a resort to military action. As it turned out, the military men on the spot behaved, on the whole, with scant regard for the nationalist sensibilities of the Asian races whom they were 'liberating.'

The military plan provided for a three-phase operation to achieve Japan's political aims. In the first phase, the armed forces would invade the territories of the Southern Resources Area, defeating the colonial

Zero fighters assembled for the start of the war in the Pacific

armies which occupied them; in the second, a defensive perimeter around this new Pacific Empire would be consolidated, and in the third, the ousted European powers would batter ineffectually against the barrier opposing their return, before settling for a compromise peace. With the benefit of hindsight, this plan appears outrageously optimistic, but given the existing situation, with the colonial powers so weakened by their struggle with Germany, with Russia concerned with her western territories rather than with her eastern neighbours, and granted that the United States, despite her enormous economic potential for war, apparently lacked the stomach to undertake it, Imperial headquarters, with the army predominating, reckoned that the operation could succeed. Certainly in the early months of the war it seemed as though the Japanese could not make a false move; their offensives progressed with a clockwork precision that disguised the rigidity of their overall planning and the basic weaknesses in their military machine.

The Pacific War started with six practically simultaneous operations in widely separated areas. Nearest to the Japanese homeland, Hong Kong was attacked, its Commonwealth garrison surrendering on Christmas Day, Pearl Harbor was rendered temporarily powerless after a whirlwind air assault, the US bases at Guam and Wake were rapidly subjugated, Malaya was attacked and the invasion of the Philippines began. Somewhat later the Japanese started their assault on Burma, where operations were in the hands of General Iida's Fifteenth Army which had previously occupied Siam. Fifteenth Army's early attacks were directed against the Tenasserim airfields on that long strip of territory shared with Siam which connects the Malayan peninsula with mainland South-East Asia. With the northern flank thus secured for the forces attacking down to Singapore, Iida turned his army first against the port of Moulmein and then moved north to take Burma's capital and major sea port, Rangoon. With Rangoon secured, and the occupying forces reinforced by two fresh divisions, Iida pushed the ill-equipped British forces up the Irrawaddy and Sittang valleys and chased the two Chinese armies which Chiang Kai-Shek had put into Burma across the Salween river and back into China. When the monsoon broke General Alexander's Burma Army was back in north-eastern India and the Chinese on the Salween front were deprived of their sole land lifeline to their allies, the Burma Road.

On the map, the republic of Burma has the appearance of a diamond-shaped wedge whose northern half has been pushed between the huge land masses of India and China which flank it. By comparison with her giant neighbours Burma appears deceptively small, an impression rapidly dispelled when one realises that Rangoon and Fort Hertz, at the southern and northern ends respectively of Burma proper, are as far apart as Marseilles in southern France and York in northern England, and that the alternating hills and valleys of this rugged country occupy a total of 240,000 square miles, an area greater than that of France and Belgium combined, while its coastline, fronting

the Indian Ocean with mangrove swamps and scattered jungly islands, stretches for 1,200 miles. When the Japanese invaded it in 1942 Burma was a strangely isolated land, with only a few hill trails connecting it with Assam State in India and with southern Siam to the east. On Burma's western flank, a long finger of mountain hooks down from the end of the Himalayas creating a natural frontier barrier with India before it peters out as the low but spiney-backed hills called the Arakan Yoma. To the east a more extensive Himalayan protrusion, the Yunnan plateau, provides the frontier with China, while further south this plateau land becomes a more specific mountain range which effectively delineates the border with Siam. The only significant man-made highway which traversed either of these natural borders in 1942 was the famous Burma Road, which ran northwards from the mud flats of the estuary at Rangoon to the Old Burma capital of Mandalay, and thence swinging eastwards and rapidly gaining height it pushed across the border into mountainous Yunnan.

The building of a similar road across Burma's western frontier into India would have been a difficult engineering feat, but it would also have been superfluous, for Burma easily maintained a flourishing trade with India via Rangoon. In 1942, as now, Rangoon was the key to the penetration of Burma. The three great rivers of Burma, the Salween, the Chindwin and the Irrawaddy flow down from the mountainous north to Rangoon, the railway which ran through the central corridor of Burma terminated at Rangoon. Rangoon was the industrial centre, the oil refinery of Burma and through its well-developed docks passed the bulk of the goods which she imported, and the rice, oil, wolfram and timber which she exported in return. It was not surprising therefore that the capture of Rangoon provided the key to General Iida's occupation of the

Above: After the surrender. Japanese armour in Singapore city. *Below:* The Rangoon docks are taken over after the capture of the city

country, or that his reinforcing divisions came by sea to this port rather than trekking laboriously across from central Siam as the spearhead forces had done. Burma was thus a giant cul-de-sac, entered with ease at the Rangoon gateway, but leading nowhere. It may thus seem strange that in June 1942 Imperial General Headquarters in Tokyo should have ordered HQ Southern Army, responsible for all the South East Asian territories, to build a railway from Siam to Burma as a substitute for the sea route to Rangoon.

The decision to undertake such a formidable engineering task, to push a railroad through an area composed for the most part of tropical rain forest, fast flowing rivers and the old, hard rocks of a mountain range, was not made lightly. It stemmed essentially from the strains which the attempt to defend and exploit the new Pacific Empire was putting on Japan's already limited naval resources, particularly those of her merchant marine. Japan's greatest asset in the war was the fighting spirit of her military forces, and it was upon their courage, tenacity and physical endurance rather than on a preponderance of any material military resource that she came increasingly to rely. In December 1941 she had committed only eleven of her fifty-one divisions, less than 200,000 men in all, to the conquest of the Philippines, Malaya, Burma and the Dutch East Indies, and her naval forces were used, like the land divisions, successively for different tasks. But while the initial conquests proved a relatively easy task, the almost contemptuous ease with which Japan made them tended to obscure, for a time at least, her glaring strategic weaknesses. The subsequent defence of such a vast area as she had acquired proved immeasurably more difficult than she had imagined, for not only had Imperial HQ to arrange the supply and reinforcement of her widespread garrisons, scattered over many thousands of square miles, but her merchant marine had to set about the enormous task of importing to Japan the essential raw materials for her war industries as well as transporting back shiploads of military *matériel*. The development of this economic exchange was, after all, the *raison d'être* of the 'Greater East Asia Co-prosperity Sphere', and the weakness of her merchant marine was to prove to be Japan's Achilles' heel.

During the 1930s Japan's merchant fleet had been enormously improved and enlarged so that by 1940 it consisted of over 700 ocean-going freighters, 132 passenger-cargo vessels and forty-four ocean-going tankers. But in 1941 it still totalled only six million tons; thirty-five per cent of Japan's imports continued to be carried under the flag of other nations. Nor were her naval yards capable of any rapid expansion of the merchant fleet building programme; Japan had earlier denounced the Washington Naval Treaty on fleet limitations and from 1937 onwards the requirements of her expanding navy meant that civilian yards were switched from the construction of merchant vessels to building destroyers, battleships and carriers. Thereafter, her merchant shipping authority lacked the staff, the experience and the prestige to promote a large-scale expansion of the merchant fleet, competing as it was with the peremptory demands of the influential Imperial navy. For these reasons, the Japanese found it increasing difficult to furnish the shipping lanes of the new empire with an adequate supply of vessels, and on no route was this difficulty more keenly felt than on the long haul to Rangoon.

The first part of the sea route to Rangoon was, of course, quite direct, passing through the East and South China Seas, but then came the long detour around the Malay peninsula to Singapore, and thence up the narrow Malacca Strait and through

To Aleutian Is.

PACIFIC OCEAN

Pearl Harbor **Hawaii**

Midway

Society Is.

Phoenix Is.

Tokelau

W. Samoa

Tonga

Fiji Is.

Marshall Is.

Makin

Gilbert Is.

Wake

Eniwetok

Kwajalein

Tarawa

Ellice Is.

New Hebrides

New Caledonia

Solomon Is.

Bougainville

Guadalcanal AUG. 1942

Rabaul

Bismarck Arch.

Truk

Caroline Islands

Port Moresby

NEW GUINEA

LIMIT OF JAPANESE EXPANSION, JULY 1942

Marianas Is.

Saipan

Tinian

Guam

Yap

Palau

HOKKAIDO

JAPAN

Tokyo

HONSHU

SHIKOKU

KYUSHU

Iwo Jima

Okinawa

Ryukyu Is.

FORMOSA

Kurile Is.

MANCHURIA

KOREA

Dairen

Shanghai

Hong Kong

PHILIPPINE IS.

LUZON

Leyte

MINDANAO

Morotai

CELEBES

Timor

Darwin

MONGOLIA

C H I N A

Chungking

THAI-LAND

FR. INDO-CHINA

BURMA

INDIA

MALAYA

Singapore

SUMATRA

BORNEO

DUTCH EAST INDIES

Batavia

AUSTRALIA

Alice Springs

Mercator Projection

the Andaman Sea to Rangoon. Not only was this detour long, it was also dangerous, for the Strait of Malacca marked the limit of Japan's defensive perimeter: beyond it lay the Indian Ocean and British India. Just as Japan had placed too much reliance upon the martial qualities of her fighting soldiers, so also she had underestimated the resilience of her opponents; it was from the Indian sub-continent that one prong of the counteroffensive against her was to come. Even in early 1942 the vulnerability of her sea traffic along the narrow and predictable last lap of its journey to Burma was being demonstrated, several vessels having already succumbed to submarine attack off the west coast of Malaya and in the Andaman Sea. Elsewhere in the Pacific she was also sustaining losses to her merchant fleet; by June 1942, before the Allied submarine campaign had really started, she had already lost ninety-one merchant ships, a total of over 400,000 tons of valuable cargo space, while in June itself came her defeat at Midway and the loss of four aircraft carriers. Japan's ability to use the sea at will and to prevent her opponents from using it was already being severely restricted; merchant shipping had consequently to be carefully utilised.

The switch to Bangkok as the terminus for the sea traffic to Burma was consequently a logical decision, since it would not only avoid vulnerable areas of sea where Japanese naval strength could be contested, albeit only by submarines and aircraft in early 1942, but it would also reduce the line of communication to General Iida's army by over 1,200 miles, an immense saving in fuel and time for the hard-pressed merchant fleet. The only difficulty was that Bangkok was separated from the well-developed Burma railway system by over 250 miles of primitive, rugged terrain, an area so inhospitable that few Thais or Burmese chose to live there, drenched as it was by a five-month

monsoon and endemically malarial. Before the war, European engineers had conducted a preliminary survey for just such a railway project linking Burma with Siam as the Japanese were now contemplating. Their conclusion was that although a rail connection between the two countries was practicable, engineering and other difficulties would prevent it from being an economic proposition. Japan's engineering resources, both military and civil, were already strained and the absence of a local labour force presented another difficulty. The Japanese engineers who

now examined the railway project therefore opined that it would take five or six years to complete, a time-span much too lengthy for the impatient demands of war. There was, however, another factor which made the idea of a Burma-Siam railway a more realistic possibility.

Scattered in prisons and improvised camps throughout Malaya, Singapore, Java and Sumatra were tens of thousands of Allied prisoners of war whose existence was both an embarrassment and an encumbrance to the Japanese military forces. As a Japanese interpreter put it to one group of prisoners, it would have been more satisfactory if they had all allowed themselves to be killed in battle rather than be taken prisoner. It seems certain that the capture of such a huge and largely unwounded military force came as a surprise to the Imperial army; a surprise because the possibility of being taken prisoner was not something which the Japanese soldier ever considered. His function was to fight for the Emperor, unto death if need be, for

Japanese freighter under attack in the Andaman Sea

there was no greater honour than to die for the Emperor, nor any worse dishonour than to be taken prisoner. The Allied prisoners were also an encumbrance since the Japanese had now to undertake the chore of feeding them. It seemed degrading for victors to have to provide sustenance for a dishonoured and disgraced enemy, but Japan's adherence to various international conventions apparently made it necessary. That this unwanted mass of labour should be used to build the projected railway seemed logical; as prisoners the men had surely ceased to exist in the minds of the people in their homelands, as would Japanese similarly placed; they could now be given a chance to live again in the service of Tenno Heika, the Emperor of Nippon. Besides, the removal of thousands of European prisoners from the areas where they had previously ruled as white overlords, to an inaccessible part of Siam would considerably ease the security problem; 54,000 unwounded soldiers in Malaya and Singapore, and many more in Java and Sumatra could be a menace if they were able to re-establish their old contacts, particularly with the local Chinese who were known to detest the invaders and who were already supporting guerilla bands in the jungle. In Siam it would be impossible for them to escape, for even given the necessary strength and the determination, there was nowhere to escape to, the nearest Allied forces were nearly 1,000 miles away beyond dense jungle and no help could be expected from the local natives, while the forays of the Japanese fleet had driven friendly naval forces far from the coastal seas of Siam. Moreover, the 'ricebowl' of Burma and Siam could much more easily provide food for a large labour force than could Malaya or Singapore.

However, it was not administrative convenience but vital strategic considerations which most influenced the decision to go ahead with the Burma-Siam railway project. Burma was important to Japan in part because of its raw materials, namely timber, oil and tungsten ore and its annual rice surplus of which Japan's population stood urgently in need, but more particularly because it constituted the north-western bastion of the defensive ring which she had thrown around her Southern Resources Area. Unlike the other areas which completed this perimeter, Burma had a land frontier with the territory that was a main Allied eastern base, British India, which had for centuries been the foundation from which British influence had spread throughout the Far East. It was essential for the Japanese to hold Burma strongly on the line of the Chindwin river and to be able to reinforce this front quickly, for if the Allied forces could once penetrate to southern Burma, to an area where they might have a better line of communication than that through the mountainous Indo-Burmese border and across the wide and bridgeless Brahmaputra, the whole Japanese position in South East Asia would be undermined. But as things stood in 1942 Japanese communications within Burma were good, whereas the British communications from their forward positions in Assam to the main centres of India proper were execrable. As its supply lines General Iida's army had first of all the great rivers which were Burma's traditional highways: the Irrawaddy, navigable from its delta at Rangoon up to Myitkyina 1,000 miles from the sea, its tributary the Chindwin which could take river traffic for over 600 miles of its course, and the Sittang, shorter and flowing parallel with the Irrawaddy from central Burma down to the estuary near Rangoon. For years these rivers had carried the timber trade from the jungles of the north to the yards and processing plants in the Rangoon area.

There were also excellent railway links between the main population

Above: Propaganda photo of POWs captured in Singapore. *Below:* Ceremonial arrival at Singapore station of first Japanese-run train on the Malayan Railway

centres, the main line running from Pegu in the delta to Myitkyina, the terminus of the river traffic. From this main line branches pushed out to either side of the central plain of Burma, while in the south a branch line connected Rangoon and Pegu with a line running from Moulmein to Ye at the northern end of the Tenasserim peninsula. But at Ye the line stopped, south-east of it lay over 200 miles of mountain watershed before the plain of southern Siam was reached, and the nodal railway station at Ban Pong, from which town tracks stretched east and south, linking the systems of Malaya and Singapore with those that straddled Siam. All that was needed to give the Japanese a communication system to link her forces in Singapore, Malaya and Siam with those in Burma, together with a much shorter sea route to the Burma front, was a stretch of track linking Ban Pong on the Bangkok-Singapore line with some point on the Moulmein-Ye line. It was this route that the engineers of Southern Army Railway Corps now set out to plan.

The route chosen for the track followed an old British survey line abandoned before the war because of the difficulties involved. It led north from Ban Pong along the east bank of the Mae Khlong river to the latter's junction with the river Khwae Noi. The track was to cross the Mae Khlong just north of the confluence and then hug the east bank of the Khwae Noi until the river finally petered out in a mass of tributary streams in the mountains to the north; thence the line would cross the border into Burma at the lofty Three Pagodas Pass before snaking down the other side of the hills to an anticipated junction with the Ye-Moulmein railway at Thanbyuzayat, a village about fifty miles north of Ye. The construction difficulties were formidable but the chosen route did have certain advantages: the river, whose course it followed, could be used for the transport of construction materials and supplies, and an asphalt road already skirted the chosen route for about forty miles before it degenerated into little more than an earth track leading to the hills through thickening jungle.

The engineers planned to commence work at both ends of the line simultaneously, using Thanbyuzayat and Ban Pong as the first base camps for their labour forces which worked to the orders of the 5th Railway Regiment located at Thanbyuzayat or the 9th, based at Kanchanaburi where the Railway Corps also had its headquarters. From the base camps parties of prisoners would move up-country, constructing bases for the groups which were to follow them, hacking a rough trace for the engineers' surveys, and laying telephone lines. At this stage, the main labour forces would come up, to be set down at intervals at the camps along the route, to prepare the ground to receive the tracks which would follow along behind them. A communication road would also have to be developed for not all the materials could come up by river. The plan was straightforward enough, but its execution was a daunting prospect. The route lay across wide rivers, mountains of solid rock and stretches of flatter country that became young lakes in the monsoon season. Each month from June to October parts of the proposed route had between thirty and fifty inches of rain emptied upon them, and in much of the area little food was available locally and malaria was endemic. Furthermore, the Japanese engineers had few of the mechanical aids which would normally be used for such a major undertaking. But there were plenty of prisoners, and the project was to be, in the neutral words of the economists, 'labour intensive'.

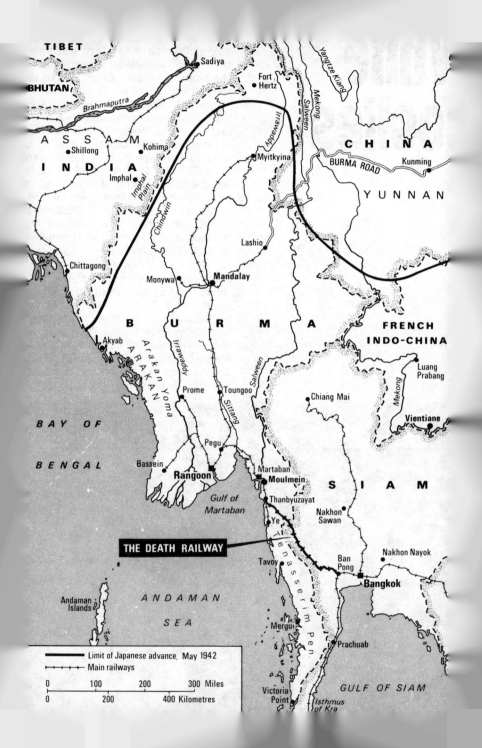

TIBET

BHUTAN

• Sadiya

Fort
Hertz

A S S A M

Brahmaputra

C H I N A

Yangtze Kiang

Mekong

Salween

• Shillong

• Kohima

• Myitkyina

BURMA ROAD

Kunming

I N D I A

Imphal •
*Imphal
Plain*

Y U N N A N

Chindwin

• Lashio

Chittagong

Monywa •

• **Mandalay**

B U R M A

FRENCH
INDO-CHINA

Akyab

Arakan Yoma

ARAKAN

Irrawaddy

Salween

Luang
Prabang

Prome •

• Toungoo

Sittang

• Chiang Mai

Mekong

Vientiane

B A Y   O F

Pegu •

B E N G A L

Bassein •

Rangoon

Martaban •
Moulmein

*Gulf of
Martaban*

Thanbyuzayat

S I A M

Nakhon
Sawan

Ye •

THE DEATH RAILWAY

Tenasserim Pen.

Nakhon Nayok

Tavoy •

Ban
Pong

A N D A M A N

Bangkok

Andaman
Islands

S E A

Mergui •

Prachuab •

——— Limit of Japanese advance, May 1942
+-+-+ Main railways

Victoria
Point

GULF OF SIAM

0   100   200   300 Miles

0   200   400 Kilometres

*Isthmus
of Kra*

White coolies

The Allied prisoners were, of course, not privy to the Japanese plans; they were sufficiently occupied with the basic business of survival in their temporary camps throughout the region. In April 1942 the future railway force was concentrated in four main areas: Pudu Jail in Malaya's capital of Kuala Lumpur, the Changi area of Singapore, a series of camps near Batavia in Java, and at Padang on the west coast of Sumatra. The bulk of the prisoners were in Singapore, where on 15th February 1942 General Percival, commanding 56,000 British and Australian troops and 60,000 Indians, had ordered a surrender to General Yamashita's invading army. Two days later, carrying rations for ten days and a minimum of equipment, the British and Australian prisoners had been marched out of Singapore city to the Changi area in the north east of the island, thereby losing contact with their Indian troops who had been sent to separate camps. Conditions rapidly deterio-

rated; stocks of service rations began to run low and were replaced by a monotonous diet of rice to which European stomachs were unaccustomed, and which, lacking in protein as it was, began the rapid process of debilitation which was to be the permanent condition of many of the prisoners until the end of the war. At Changi the POWs were left very much to themselves; a perimeter fence was erected but within it they were responsible for their own administration which continued, for a time at least, on the same unit basis as had existed before the surrender. In the early days at Changi many prisoners saw very little of their captors, but after a few weeks the POW administration had to provide working parties for tasks on various parts of the island where, among other things they cleared war damage, disposed of mines, built roads, worked at the docks and constructed, at Bukit Timah, a shrine to the Fallen Warriors of Japan.

For many of the prisoners these working parties provided their first opportunity to size up their captors at close quarters, and the experience was not an edifying one. The Japanese worked the prisoners hard, provided the same meagre, rice-based diet and subjected them to beatings for any failure to obey orders. The camps for the outside working parties were primitive affairs and in general the only basic amenities which they possessed were those installed by the prisoners themselves, often with materials they stole when out in different parts of the island working in labour gangs. Few drugs were provided for the increasing number of men who fell ill, and because of the need to provide working parties of a specific size, many sick men were forced out to work alongside their healthier comrades. Yet despite the strenuous work, insanitary accommodation and

Disarmed British troops are marched off to captivity

the risk of beatings, there was seldom a lack of volunteers for the working parties since it gave men a chance of a change of scenery, an opportunity to gather up-to-date news and, more importantly, the chance to steal food and medicines or else to buy these valuable commodities with their remaining valuables or pay.

Allied soldiers who had been captured during the fighting withdrawal through the length of Malaya were at first kept in compounds or prisons near to their place of surrender, but gradually they were concentrated in the civilian prison in Kuala Lumpur, Pudu Jail, which became the central POW Camp in Malaya for European captives. The initial plight of the 1,200 prisoners incarcerated there was much worse than that of their comrades in Singapore, for while many of the latter became prisoners with their equipment intact or easily accessible, those in Malaya had either been captured in battle or picked up later behind the lines while trying to escape. Their worldly goods consisted only of what they stood up in, most were exhausted and hungry, and some wounded. Pudu Jail became severely overcrowded, its makeshift hospital being at times so pressed that it could only accommodate the desperately ill. The Japanese organisation was chaotic and for a time they used only a fraction of the space available with the result that during the day more than 700 men were crammed into what in peacetime had been an exercise yard for thirty female prisoners. During six months at Pudu about 100 of its inmates died, many of them men whose units had earlier achieved the only successes in the general gloom of the disastrous Malayan campaign. After a few months the conditions in the jail improved somewhat, the rations got better though they remained rice-based, and the Japanese opened up another section of the compound, so that its three sections which formed a crude 'Y' now housed Australian prisoners in

one arm, Asiatics and civilians in the other, and the captured British troops in the stem. Working parties moved out from Pudu, engaged in similar tasks to those in Singapore and activated by a similar philosophy: making as much use of their limited freedom as possible to improve their diet, and doing only enough work to avoid a beating from the Japanese labour gangers. In both Malaya and Singapore the Japanese authorities attempted to make use of the technical knowledge of their prisoners by employing them to repair equipment or broken-down lorries. A questionnaire on trades and professional qualifications was circulated to prisoners in Kuala Lumpur in an attempt by the Japanese to rationalise their use of the labour force. The fact that so many prisoners could still claim to be 'beer testers', 'brothel inspectors' or 'centenary bell

Above: The crowded conditions of Selarang Barracks in Singapore. *Below:* A hut of the type used at Changi to accommodate up to 250 men.

Above: The cookhouse at Selarang
Right: The US heavy cruiser *Houston*
Below: The Australian light cruiser
Perth.

ringers' testifies to their continuing good humour after several months of strenuous labour, poor medical treatment and the unvarying and inadequate diet.

The bulk of the prisoners captured on Java had spent an equally unpleasant early captivity, the general atmosphere on this, the most populous island of the Dutch East Indies was extremely forbidding, with the majority of the native population violently anti-European. The prisoner force consisted in the main of the 8,000 British and Australian troops who had made up its Commonwealth garrison at the surrender, and the many Dutch, military and civilian personnel, who were also taken prisoner. To these were added the survivors from Allied ships sunk off Java, in particular hundreds of sailors from the USS *Houston* and HMAS *Perth*, the two Allied cruisers which, while trying to escape from the Java Sea, sailed into the midst of a huge Japanese naval force which was in the process of invading Batavia. A grim but hopelessly uneven night action followed under a full moon until both ships finally went down,

Above: The cookhouse at Selarang
Right: The US heavy cruiser *Houston*
Below: The Australian light cruiser
Perth.

taking hundreds of their crew members with them, and leaving the survivors to swim ashore and spend the next three and a half years in prison camps. During the first weeks of captivity many of the prisoners had a fair degree of freedom in the areas in which they had surrendered in the western half of the island, but this was not the case for those who were incarcerated in the cinema at Serang, among them the survivors from the two Allied cruisers. Here 1,500 prisoners, with numerous wounded, were squeezed into the small auditorium which seated only 500 locals at a 'full house'. There were no washing facilities, food consisted of a small issue of poor quality rice and medical treatment for the wounded was completely lacking. Many of the sailors were still covered with fuel oil from the ships which stung their eyes and blocked the pores. Some were later transferred to Serang jail which became just as overcrowded with thirty-four men occupying each

cell built for eight native prisoners. When these captives were finally transferred to the old Dutch barracks known as the 'Bicycle Camp,' the majority were already suffering from acute malnutrition and claustrophobia and many had dysentery or chronic diarrhoea. Even during the later horrors on the railway the men who had campaigned in the Serang cinema and jail were known by the prestigious title of 'old Dysenterians.'

Many of the small ships which sailed from Singapore in the last days before the island surrendered were sunk or captured in the narrow Banka Strait off the east coast of Sumatra. Some parties were fortunate enough to make their way overland across to the west coast before capture, and here a group of 500 British prisoners were collected who were also to form part of the labour force for the Burma-Siam railway. Altogether, scattered about the area, in Malaya, Singapore and the East Indies were some 61,000 men, Australian, American, Dutch and British who were to be the railway's military labour force. By April 1942 none of them was fit for prolonged heavy work; malaria, dysentery and numerous jungle fevers and intestinal conditions were already taking their toll, some were developing jungle sores, others pellagra, while those whom these scourges had not yet visited were rapidly losing weight and some of their number were subject to temporary blackouts. Meanwhile, the course of the next two years of their lives was being plotted by the Japanese engineers and staff officers who were responsible for the establishment of the line of communication to General Iida's Fifteenth Army in Burma.

The first POW labour forces to move north to Burma and Siam left their camps in Changi, Batavia and Padang in April and May 1942, just as the south-west monsoon was beginning to break. The group known in Singapore as 'A' Force, 3,000 Australians from Changi under Brigadier Varley, made the journey up to Burma by sea, one of the first of the 'hell ship' journeys with which many more prisoners were later to be familiar. The men were crammed into the airless and insanitary holds of Japanese freighters where the rapid spread of tropical infections was unavoidable. 'A' Force worked initially on the airfields of southern Burma at Victoria Point, Tavoy and Mergui before moving to the site of the railway later

Propaganda photograph of prisoners exercising

in the year. They were joined in the airfield repair work by the British (Sumatra) battalion, formed from the prisoners who had been collected at Padang. While these groups were on the move the Japanese were also organising advance parties in Singapore for despatch to the Siamese end of the project. When the news of a possible move percolated through to the prisoners at Changi, many looked forward to it, hoping for better food and a more congenial environment than that provided by the island's camps. Disillusionment came swiftly with the journey by rail from Singapore station, which was made in small steel box cars into each of which about thirty men were crammed. The overcrowding was such that lying down was out of the question, it was impossible even to sit until the bundles of belongings were stuffed to one side, and even then in some of the more crowded trucks a roster had to be devised by which each prisoner had a period of standing and then of sitting down. For five days and nights the trains rattled over the narrow gauge rails

until finally they reached their destination at Ban Pong, the point from
which the new railway was to start.

Ban Pong lay in the flat agricultural plain of southern Siam, rich in
rice and in a variety of tropical fruit:
its only significance in these early
days was that it was the station at
which the railway from Singapore,
running due north and hugging the
east coast of the Tenasserim peninsula, swung sharply right before com-

pleting the last fifty miles of its
journey to Bangkok. The prisoners
did not go on to Bangkok, instead
they climbed wearily from the steel
trucks at Ban Pong, stretched their
legs properly for the first time in
almost five days, and looked about
them. They had arrived at the village
which was to be the first of the great
staging posts on the railway project;
over the course of the next year
many thousands of conscripted

labourers would pass through it *en route* to destinations further north. The prisoners' camp at Ban Pong had the advantage of lying alongside the dwellings of the town and the men were able to begin a brisk trade with the Thai villagers, bartering their few valuables for fruit, eggs and palm sugar. Parker pens and watches were always in great demand, but while these often changed hands at a rate of barter that gave the Thais a handsome profit, their loss to the prisoners was much less than that of items of clothing which were also sold, and particularly of mosquito nets, later to be priceless possessions in the insect-ridden jungle camps. This trade was only possible because the men were seldom closely guarded in and around the camps themselves until much later in the war. Indeed, in many of the less accessible camps the Japanese guards themselves acted as middlemen in the barter trade.

Ban Pong gave the advance parties their first sight of the kind of accommodation they were to occupy for the rest of their internment (except for the not infrequent occasions when they would have no roof over their heads at all). The new dwellings were atap huts, primitive wooden structures of bamboo and leaves, in shape not unlike ridge pole tents with low sides. Their construction was simple and employed only the natural products of the jungle, bamboo, atap leaves and lashings made from the stringy underbark of trees. The building of atap huts was quite a skilled business and required a good deal of practice and many prisoners became adept at the art before their time on the railway was over. Long bamboo poles were first inserted into the ground like tent poles, forming the pillars for the structure, then other bamboos were laid across them to form the ridge of the huts, to which others were attached as roof supports. Many huts had no side walls as such, the roofs merely sloping down close to the ground. The roof covering was made from atap leaves laid across thin bamboo laths, like so many flexible, overlapping tiles, each being wound and laid individually on the cross-pieces. The hut furniture was simple in the extreme and consisted only of two low platforms, one running down the length of each side of the hut. These too were of the universal bamboo and stood a couple of feet from the ground. They formed the beds for the prisoners, each of whom would occupy about two feet of lateral space, practically touching his immediate neighbours. This was where the labourers were to get fresh energy for the next day's tasks, lying in serried ranks along bamboo platforms. On occasions there were as many as 200 men to a hut.

However, Ban Pong was not in any sense a typical railway camp, its proximity to Bangkok and the availability of local food supplies ensured that the prisoners there had a chance to supplement the meagre diet which the Japanese provided, and to purchase some of the medical supplies which they did not have. Nor did the actual railway construction in the immediate area of Ban Pong present the formidable problems that were to be confronted up-country. For the first twenty miles, the trace passed over relatively flat ground and required only the shifting of earth to form a small embankment before rock chippings were added for ballast and the lines laid. From Ban Pong the trace skirted the wooded banks of the wide and meandering Mae Khlong river until it reached the town of Kanchanaburi and the village of Tamarkan a couple of miles further on. Here it was to cross the as yet unbridged Mae Khlong before it continued up the east bank of the River Khwae Noi which it followed up to the river's source. Beyond Tamarkan the land rose steadily in height, became more rugged, jungle-clad and infinitely more fearsome as a route to be travelled even on foot, let alone as the track for a railway. Here bridges would have to be built over the scores of tiny tributary streams that ran into the Khwae Noi, a track would have to be driven along the sides of mountains, and where one rock feature fell sheer away culverts and viaducts would have to span the yawning gap to the next. Before most of this exacting labour could even be attempted a stretch of primary jungle would have to be cleared, towering hardwood trees laboriously sawn down and clumps of the stubborn and ubiquitous bamboo patiently uprooted stem by stem.

But these tasks were in the future, the advance parties of prisoners had other labours to occupy them under the direction of their Nipponese masters, who now began to take a greater interest in their activities than had been shown on the journey up from Singapore. The Japanese personnel charged with the supervision of this mammoth task were of two distinct types. First there were the trained, skilled and intelligent railway engineers whose function was to plan, survey and direct the project. Some of them were educated men with a good command of English, but such humanitarian instincts as the Japanese engineers possessed were pushed aside by their single-minded determination to have the railway completed on time, the target date for which was November 1943. They were not in any case the direct masters of the POWs, who were in the charge of administrative troops whose responsibility was to guard and feed them as well as seeing that they worked at their appointed tasks. This latter Japanese group was of poor quality; many of its officers were incompetent, while some of its other ranks were moronic and at times almost bestial in their treatment of the prisoners. This applied particularly to the Korean private soldiers, conscripted only for guard and sentry duties in many parts of the new Japanese empire and regrettably appointed as guards for the prisoners in many of the camps in Burma and Siam.

Since the staging camp at Ban Pong was already prepared when the advance parties arrived there in May 1942, they were soon moved north again to build fresh camps along the trace. Many went by lorry on this next leg of the journey, along the all-weather road that stretched as far as the junction of the two rivers. The road ran past the town of Kanchanaburi, an ancient trading post previously little visited by European travellers, but soon to have thousands of them trudging past its brick and wooden shacks. It was a surprisingly well developed town for an area which was otherwise little advanced, and boasted temples, government bungalows and a ruined fort as well as two modern factories for processing timber. Located near the confluence of the rivers, Kanchanaburi was ideally placed for the collection of logs floated down from the forested areas. It was largely because of the town's good communications that the Japanese chose it as the headquarters for the Southern Army Railway Corps.

The advance parties were soon moving on from Kanchanaburi, being herded on to barges at the riverside near Tamarkan and pulled across to the west bank of the river by small native motor boats known as 'pom-poms.' The Mae Khlong was now left behind and the planned course of the railway swung westwards alongside the Khwae Noi, the other major waterway. A few miles west of the river junction the prisoners found themselves at the tented camp of Chungkai where their task was the erection of atap huts for a much larger labour force. Chungkai was destined to be one of the major bases for the jungle section of the operations controlled from the Siamese end. Rafts of bamboo moored at the riverside were broken up and dragged to the camp site where the prisoners were initiated, to the accompaniment of frequent beatings, into the mysteries of erecting atap huts sixty yards

long without the aid of a single nail, and with only a saw or axe to trim the bamboo and fashion rough holes for the pillar pieces. Thatching the roofs with atap leaves was the most tedious part of the work since every leaf had to be tied separately and overlapping its neighbour if the whole structure was to keep out the tropical downpour which engulfed the railroad area for five months each year. Prisoners who moved up to Siam later on were to curse the inadequate roofings built on these early huts by their inexperienced comrades in the advance parties.

As the weeks went by activity extended northwards along the river bank as more camp spaces were cleared and huts erected. The work became steadily more difficult as the

Left: POW's journey up-river on a crowded barge. *Below:* 100-yard-long prison huts at Chungkai camp

vegetation changed from the dreary expanses of paddy to the bamboo thickets and forest-covered hills across the Mae Khlong, and then to the jungle-clad mountains further up-country. While some prisoners cleared the camps, others humped sacks of rice and engineer stores from the barges which plied up and down the river life-line, and further parties started to clear a rough track for lorries alongside the railway trace. The jungle camps had a depressing similarity; always the same atap huts, and inevitably one or two of them set aside as a hospital, not that the word 'hospital' necessarily had much significance. All that could with certainty be said about these buildings was that they contained desperately sick men and that they were attended by a prisoner medical officer whose treatment consisted mainly of words of encouragement. The patients were spared, however, the exertions of the railroad gangs. In these early days at least, when the diet at the base camps nearer to the agricultural districts of Siam was still reasonably nourishing many sick men had a fair chance of recovery. The huts in which they were housed, plus a makeshift cookhouse area and a latrine pit formed the bare bones of the camps, set apart from which would be the more spacious and better constructed quarters for the Japanese guards, and of course a crude camp guard room.

Work proceeded slowly at first for the advance parties were small and not all of them worked directly on the railway but on other tasks, while at the Burma end the project had hardly been started for the first draft of Australians was still labouring at the repair and development of the Tenasserim airfields. In October, however, the main parties started to move up from Changi and Batavia. For the Changi prisoners a move of some kind came as no surprise, the possibility of other drafts following the advance parties had already been

Left: A hospital hut at Chungkai. *Above:* Improvised camp cookhouse with clay ovens and 4-gallon petrol tins for boiling water. *Below:* A POW's impression of the 'Selarang Barracks Incident'

discussed, and since then other groups had been shipped off to Japan and to other parts of the 'Co-prosperity Sphere,' including all the officers of the rank of colonel and above, and the senior civil servants, who had been sent to Formosa. However, the move of individual groups came abruptly and their destination was not disclosed to them by the camp guards. At this stage many of the prisoners looked forward to the change, particularly since the Singapore prisoners had recently suffered the notorious 'Selarang Barracks Incident' when 15,400 officers and men had been herded into the parade square and adjacent buildings of Selarang Barracks, designed to accommodate a single battalion, and kept there until they agreed to sign individual undertakings not to attempt to escape from Japanese captivity. Since the appalling and insanitary overcrowding was already producing sickness, the senior POW officers agreed to sign after three days of confinement in this latter-day Black Hole of Calcutta.

In September a Red Cross ship had arrived in Singapore, so the parties which moved off in early October did at least get a few tins of food, a pair of boots each and a hat before they started the journey. The move up was again made by rail, in the same steel trucks and with similar acute discomfort, for the waggons were again grossly overcrowded and became as hot as ovens during the heat of the day when only a small area near the central sliding door of each truck gave any relief from the stifling atmosphere inside. This space would be occupied by turns to give each man a chance to cool off, but most often it was reserved for the dysentery and diarrhoea sufferers whose plight neither exempted them from the labour force, nor permitted them to wait for the infrequent stops on the journey when they could use the station latrines. They had consequently to hang precariously backwards out of the open doorway of the swaying trucks, gripping the door jambs as they obeyed the numerous calls of nature that were the curse of these diseases.

The men who had formed the original working parties sent to various labouring jobs around Singapore were among the first to make the journey up to Siam. Generally, battalions which had been kept together after the surrender made the trip as a complete group, but, of course, the trains were not designed to transport whole units and many had to leave part of their complement behind, sometimes to rejoin them later on, but frequently never to see them again until the Japanese surrendered. This splitting-up of closely-knit units, bound together by the ties of regimental tradition and the comradeship of adversity, was both distressing to the men themselves and damaging to their morale. It was later observed that units which managed to keep together throughout their days on the railway seemed better able to withstand the hardship and suffering which were their daily lot, than those groups of men who had been thrown together by the vagaries of the generally chaotic Japanese administration, and who had to develop ties of discipline and comradeship at the very time when their calamitous situation needed the prop of an already established military group to keep them from total despair.

The 1,000 mile rail journey was a more severe ordeal for those who had spent all their confinement hitherto within the Changi perimeter where conditions were comparatively good. Men on the outside working parties had at least had the experience of primitive accommodation and strenuous labour as mental and physical preparation for the ordeal ahead, and some preparation was certainly needed for the scenes which greeted them at the base camps in southern Siam. The monsoon rains had been raging for five months since the advance parties had first arrived, and a depressing transformation had been wrought in the low-lying camps which dotted the first stretch of the railway trace. One party arrived at Ban Pong in early October to find that their accommodation consisted of eight of the ubiquitous atap huts, all of which betrayed evidence of poor construction, one actually collapsing on its occupants during the first night. Of the others, four were flooded to a depth of over a foot, and the water lapped against the undersides of the bamboo platforms on which the men were to sleep. As one prisoner confided to his diary, 'I am writing this lying on a camp bed on a wooden platform, beneath which flows a flood of dirty water, choked with every kind of rubbish, including filth from the nearby latrines.' The situation was made even more depressing by the fact that some parties had been expressly forbidden to take any cooking utensils with them on the journey from Singapore. Fortunately, few of the main parties stayed long at the Ban Pong railhead, where the river had burst its banks; most of them exchanged the ordeal by water for a trial by marching, as they plodded up the road to Kanchanaburi, hardly sustained by their inadequate meals, and carrying all their worldly possessions on their backs. Marches frequently lasted from dawn to dusk with the heat a terrible handicap as the rays of the sun were reflected back from the smooth tarmac surface of the road. Once across the river at Tamarkan the made-up road gave place to tracks through vegetation that soon turned into almost virgin jungle; and as the jungle thickened so the terrain grew more difficult as the railway trace pushed up to the mountain ranges which separate southern Burma from Siam. Already the labour force was being imperceptibly reduced as sick and exhausted men dropped out of the marching columns, too weak or ill to be roused by the kicks or blows from rifle butts which the guards frequently rained upon them. In the evening lorries would return to pick up the sick and take them on to the group's temporary resting place, or else they would be left with the next party coming up the line. Many would already be dead.

The earlier parties had the shorter marches which took them to cleared areas of jungle, or to already established camps where larger labour forces were needed for particularly difficult tasks. The later ones moved further on, past men already toiling at the ever lengthening embankment, or blasting rough corridors through hills that lay in the path of the trace. The further they marched the wearier and weaker they became and the more arduous became the work that awaited them at their journey's end; the jungle would be thicker, the hills higher, the camps more primitive (if they existed at all), and, more ominously, they would be further away from the base areas from which food, medical supplies and other necessaries would have to be obtained. The longer their approach march to their section of the railroad, the later in the year before they arrived at it, and the shorter would be the time-span within which their section of the track would have to be completed. It is hardly surprising that the up-country camps rapidly acquired a gruesome reputation, compared with which the Changi settlement appeared to the distorted imaginations of the toiling prisoners as a kind of holiday resort. This was certainly how Changi appeared to the 800 prisoners from Pudu Jail, Kuala Lumpur, who were transferred there without warning in November 1942. They still found that they were always hungry at Changi, but the place did have the inestimable benefit of being run by the POW officers themselves and not by the Japanese whom the prisoners seldom saw unless for some reason they had to leave the main compound. In addition, the authorities somehow managed to impose something quite close to prewar

Hospital huts flooded during the monsoon season

discipline and procedure and all manner of activities, including what came to be known as the 'Changi University' were also organised to fill in the long hours of enforced confinement. Not all the men from Pudu were able to enjoy the improved conditions in Changi, however, as 400 of them were sent direct to the railway from Kuala Lumpur. From then on Malaya held no European troops, but only thousands of Indian soldiers, disillusioned and depressed at the collapse of the military system of the white sahib whose invincibility they had previously never questioned. Some had already been suborned into joining the anti-imperialist Indian National Army, but the majority remained as prisoners in jails throughout Malaya.

Thus the camps at the Siamese end of the strategic railway project began to fill up with thousands of white captives, and as they pushed the railway trace northwards, so a similarly impressed labour force started to hack their way south from Burma. At the end of September the 3,000 Australians of 'A' force had finished their airfield work and were moved by ship to Moulmein and thence by road and rail to Thanbyuzayat. Conditions at the airfield camps had been comparatively good but they were to take a dramatic turn for the worse once the men had arrived at the railway base camp in Burma. By the end of October the base had already been considerably built up, the small Thanbyuzayat station was surrounded with store sheds, piles of sleepers, rails and materials of all kinds, while a short distance away, nearer to the coast, the usual camp of atap huts housed the headquarters of the prisoners' administration and the several hundred sick men who were already victims of a combination of insufficient food, strenuous work,

A prisoner's worldly goods: 'Jap-Happy' (loin cloth), mess tin, water bottle, mug and boots without laces

Indian National Army leader Subhas
Chandra Bose (centre front) with
Lieutenant-General Mutaguchi of
Fifteenth Army (left front)

tropical disease and harsh Japanese
treatment. In October thousands of
reinforcements for the Burma section
began to march through the Thanbyuzayat camp *en route* to their
jungle destinations, dropping off their
sick men at the hospital huts as they
passed. These reinforcements were
from Batavia in Java, and many of
them had already endured worse
horrors on their way to Burma than
they were ever to experience on the
railway.

Conditions in the Batavia camps
had been comparatively good compared to those which some of the men
had suffered in their first camps

before they were concentrated near
the capital. The 'Bicycle Camp' for
example had had only six deaths in a
force of 3,000 prisoners and health in
general was not much below normal
army standards. This respite was not
to last long however, for in September
rumours of a general break-up of the
camps began to circulate and soon
afterwards parties were collected
together and sent off by sea to Singapore. The first party left the 'Bicycle
Camp' at the end of October and others
followed at frequent intervals. The
journeys by sea to Singapore and
thence up the Strait of Malacca to
Burma were further examples of the
'hellship' voyages mentioned earlier.
The nickname was lurid but it was
hardly an exaggeration. A typical
instance was the voyage of the 5,000
ton Japanese freighter which left

Batavia's port, Tanjong Priok, on 8th October 1942. It had arrived there already partially loaded with military equipment, but the Japanese nevertheless managed to cram 1,500 prisoners into its three small holds, one of which already contained a consignment of unlashed Bren carriers. The main hold had nearly 750 prisoners forced into it with such consequent overcrowding that they had to lie down on top of each other. In these foetid ovens the men languished for ninety-six hours, receiving only one and a half pints of tea and three helpings of rice and soya soup each day. Not surprisingly the first men died less than forty-eight hours after coming on board.

The freighters discharged their human cargoes at Keppel harbour Singapore, and the prisoners had a few days of freedom and comfort at Changi before continuing their journey to Burma. Most of them also got a small quantity of the Red Cross supplies which had arrived in September, and a chance to write a brief twenty-five word message home before trucks took them back to the harbour for the next stage of their journey. Some travelled with loads of Japanese stores in the holds of the small freighters, others with Nipponese soldiers, who were likewise housed in the freight holds but on upper tiers or platforms which kept them near the hatches and the fresher air which circulated once the ships got under way.

The worst times on these journeys were the hours the men spent in the holds before the ships got moving, or after they had docked, when the holds were quite devoid of fresh air but were nevertheless invaded by swarms of mosquitos which began infecting the men with malaria, endemic to much of South East Asia, and which was to be one of their constant afflictions during the railroad days. The insanitary conditions of the ships' holds also hastened the spread of other tropical diseases while further sickness resulted from the generally filthy cooking arrangement and the putrefying meat which was supposed to provide additional nourishment for the men. Sides of meat taken on board the freighters in Singapore had come from the Cold Storage Company's deep freezes and bore date stamps as early as 1931. Since most of the ships had no refrigerators the carcases soon stank to high heaven, so that only the strongest stomachs could take the meals made from them, despite the protein deficiency from which most prisoners were suffering. One ship-load of Dutch prisoners bound for the railway had a particularly nightmarish journey, doing the trip direct without a break at Singapore and experiencing an abortive attack by a British submarine to add spice to their misery. This freighter took ten days to reach Penang island and spent a further seven stifling days there following the submarine attack during which time dysentery rapidly spread among the prisoners who were cooped-up on board throughout their twenty-two day journey to Rangoon. Already fourteen men had died and scores more were on the verge of death by the time their brief confinement in Rangoon Jail started. When the fittest men of this force left Moulmein to begin work on the railway, they left behind them 200 dead and hundreds more too sick to move, even some of those who went on to Moulmein had to be carried there and later died from the grinding work on the line. Of those left in Rangoon the tally of dead eventually totalled one sixth of the original party.

The attitude of the native people to the European prisoners who passed through their villages or set up camps near their settlements was varied. The Malays were, in general, treated reasonably well by the Japanese who regarded them as the rightful owners of Malaya, with the result that they were rather cool towards the prisoners who passed through on the way to Siam. The Thais, on the other hand, were never a subject race of the Japanese in the same sense as the other people of South-East Asia were, and thus they had a good deal more freedom. While content enough to report escaped prisoners to the Japanese for the sake of the reward offered, they were also happy to trade with the prison camps near to their villages, selling duck eggs and vegetables to the POW canteen organisations. Surprisingly friendly was the welcome given by the Burmese at Moulmein to the parties of prisoners who arrived there after the horrors of their sea passages from Java. Unwarned of the prisoners' arrival, the local people nevertheless thronged the streets to watch them pass, and disregarding the Japanese guards they ran out and pressed fruit, foodstuffs, tobacoo and cheroots into their hands. It was a sorry reflection on the much vaunted 'Co-prosperity Sphere' that the newly liberated people should show such warmth and friendliness to their erstwhile imperial masters from whose toils their fellow-Asians, the Japanese, had delivered them. No such sentiments of deliverance were felt by the Chinese of South East Asia, who lived as immigrant workers in every country of the region and generally despised the Japanese. Many prisoners had cause to thank the Chinese for acts of kindness and self-sacrifice, both during the early and brief fighting, and later during their time on the railroad.

By the end of November 1942 the Burma-based labour force was almost at its designated strength. The Japanese HQ, together with Brigadier Varley's POW administration and about 100 camp workers were at Thanbyuzayat, where the dilapidated camp hospital housed several hundred more. The original 'A' Force had now been augmented by 4,600 Dutchmen from Java and Sumatra and two large drafts of Australians and Americans from Java, as well as the 500 men of the British (Sumatra) battalion. The force was practically 10,000 strong and most of the men were now working in a dozen or more camps scattered along the railway trace from the base camp to the Three Pagodas Pass, while across the border three times as many prisoners were pushing the trace northwards to join them. A 200-mile stretch of tropical rain forest, normally inhabited by a few hardy tribespeople, fishermen and hunters, now received a new population which cursed and complained in the dialects of a dozen English counties, mixed with the drawl of Texas, the vernacular of Australian city and outback and the jarring vowels of the Dutch. Here, a wealth of expertise in scores of different trades and professions was laid aside as the Japanese demanded only the crude labour of sweating bodies, armed with the simplest of tools, to build their strategic railway to the armies defending the north-western extremity of their new Empire.

For the operation of prisoner labour forces throughout the conquered territories (and the Burma-Siam railway was only one of many projects employing captured military personnel) the Japanese relied heavily on the prisoners' own existing rank structure for the transmission of their orders and the organisation of labour gangs. This naturally put the officers in a very difficult position since they were technically required to act as the taskmasters of the working forces which were generally too weak to carry out the strenuous tasks allotted to them, tasks which, in any case, completely contravened the international agreements on the treatment of prisoners of war which Japan had agreed to observe. It had long since become apparent that such undertakings were quite meaningless to the Japanese military and that refusal to carry out an allotted task could at best lead to the handing out of a frightful beating by the enraged guards or at worst to extended torture and death. The general policy of the officers among the prisoners was therefore one of co-operation with the Japanese while at the same time endeavouring to protect the men from the beatings and other punishments which were the only inducements to labour of which the Japanese were apparently aware. The officers' position was thus a most unenviable one; to the Japanese guards he was the foreman or 'ganger', to the men he was a buffer against the brutality of their captors. It was impossible to perform both functions satisfactorily and even as the soldiers grumbled at the preferential treatment given to officers as the executive agents of the Japanese, the same officers were being slapped or beaten for minor infractions of the rules which were designed to protect sick men or cover up for deficiencies.

The guards organised their labourers in platoon gangs of about twenty men. These were called *Kumis* and the officer in charge of each *Kumi* was a *Kumicho*. Two or more *Kumis* would form a *Han*, a larger work unit under a *Hancho*, all the officers wearing armbands to designate their status. During the first period of the construction of the Burma stretch of the track officers did not work in the labour gangs themselves but operated as *Kumichos* and *Hanchos* while other officers ran the camp administration. This was a vital job; the Japanese made only the most primitive camp arrangements and the efforts of the prisoners' administration, both in terms of sanitation, medical and cooking facilities and additional food supplies, could make all the difference to the only statistic that was watched with unremitting concentration in all the railway camps – the death rate. In addition, the vestige of authority which the officers generally managed to retain both in the eyes of the Japanese as well as with their own men enabled a rudimentary framework of discipline and co-operation to be maintained, without which many camps might have degenerated into total anarchy, given the intense physical and psychological pressures to which the men were subjected.

Lieutenant-Colonel (later Brigadier) A L Varley

In the Burma camps the authorities usually agreed not to use captive officers as coolies, but this was not always possible on the southern part of the railway where most of the British officers were located and where there was a much higher proportion of officers in the camps. This situation had arisen because of the Japanese policy of separating the Indian Army officers from their native troops immediately after the capitulation in Singapore. Thus it was not long before separate officer *Kumis* were operating on the railroad, often reserved for bridge-building tasks which the Japanese perhaps thought were most suitable for *Shokos*, as officers were called by them. The bridge work was certainly no less arduous. This state of affairs did not develop without protest from the officers and it was frequently not achieved without the 'Selerang Incident' type of confrontation, the Japanese threatening to shoot the officers or alternatively their men if

they did not comply. This issue was later the subject of a novel by Pierre Boule, but the particular circumstances which the author relates are certainly fictional, indeed the now famous *Bridge over the River Kwai* never in fact existed, the railroad lay alongside the river and not across it.

Work on the railway was apportioned on a task basis, each man, for example, having the job of carrying a specified quantity of earth for the embankment during a working day, or a group having to clear so many yards of jungle or hack part of a cutting of a certain length. Markers and tapes were put out and the labourers would set about their tasks, equipped only with the most primitive tools, picks, *chunkels* (heavy native hoes common throughout Asia), spades and crude containers for carrying earth or stones. The preliminary work on most of the track was jungle clearing, for which the additional tools provided were two-handled saws, axes and rope. Mechanical power was a rarity on the railway and was only used for jobs which were quite beyond execution by human muscle. While no tasks were easy, some were preferred because, as with jungle-clearing or tree-felling work, they gave the men a chance to get away from their guards for a brief spell, or because they gave some relief from the monotony of embankment or cutting work which always proceeded under the eagle eye of the guards. Clearing areas of jungle for camps or tracks was back-breaking work, pulling out large clumps of bamboo being one of the worst tasks since they clung to the earth with a strength-sapping obstinacy. Each stalk had to be removed separately and it took ten or more men pulling on a rope to do it. Thus twenty men might spend a whole day in shifting one large clump. Tree-

Interior of officers' hut at Chungkai POW camp

Officers' hut at Nakhon Nayok

A railway cutting near Chungkai camp

felling too had its problems, starting with the difficulty of sawing through the hard-wood trunks with blunt, two-handed saws. Often a severed trunk would remain upright, secured to its fellows by a mass of creeper or intertwined branches. Three trees might consequently have to be sawn through before one could be felled. The trunks and uprooted bamboos were then dragged to the edge of the trace, making a virtually impassable entanglement.

The track for the line was almost invariably on an embankment or in a cutting, and the preparation of these added sheer tedium to an activity which demanded every ounce of energy that the prisoners' weakened bodies could muster. For embankment building the Japanese task-work system was seldom applied as its authors had intended. Instead of the desired quantity of earth being dug up and carried perhaps 100 yards to the embankment by each man in the party, some men would actually dig all day, while others would carry the spoil to the embankment either in native wickerwork baskets or else in a kind of stretcher contraption made from rice bags fixed to two wooden poles. With soft soil, a short 'carry' and a reasonably fit labour force, a metre or so a day was not an unreason-

able amount, but these preconditions seldom obtained, the soil was often rock hard and had to be broken with picks before it could be shovelled into the containers; as the work progressed the 'carry' to the embankment grew longer, and the bank itself, up which the prisoners had to climb before depositing the soil, grew higher and steeper. What was more, the prisoners became more debilitated and their numbers thinned as the camp hospitals claimed an ever-increasing part of the labour force, victims of vitamin deficiency and a host of tropical complaints.

Where high embankments were not called for, cuttings would be the order of the day, and the work process would be reversed. Frequently, the trace ran across solid rock upon which the efforts of human muscle and primitive tools could make little impression. Here the Japanese resorted to the use of explosives. Normally, boreholes for the explosives were made with a crowbar and a sledge-hammer, the hole slowly deepening, a few millimetres at a time, until it was sufficient to take an effective charge. The hole usually had to be about a metre deep, and the boring of such a hole could represent a day's

work for two men. The charge would then be detonated and fragments of rock cleared away by the labourers. The Japanese engineers took few safety precautions for these blastings and the explosions often caught the prisoners unawares, the normal hazards of the railway work now being supplemented by the danger of injury from flying rock. Most tedious of all was the task of breaking up pieces of rock by hand to form the gravelly rubble which served as ballast for the rails. This job had a particular approbrium, for it was seen, in the keen judgment of the labourers carrying out the job, as removing yet another layer of human dignity, putting them on the level of convicts in penal settlements. Earth-moving machines were never seen, though on some particularly difficult sections of the trace air compressors and jackhammers gave some relief to the weary 'hammer and tap' men. In general, however, the Japanese used only what local resources could provide; there could be no question of sending to Japan for specialised mechanical aids or railway equipment. Thus, the railway labour force was composed of prisoners captured in the region, their tools were acquired locally, the raw materials for the trace were local rock and local wood,

Elephants supplemented the prisoner labour force

even the rails themselves came from the neighbouring area, and the southern part of the track came from Malaya and the northern part from Burma.

The main Malayan line on the Singapore-Bangkok route ran up the west coast of Malaya, crossing later to the east to join up with the line to the Siamese port of Singora, but there was also a branch line which traversed the central highlands of Malaya, starting at Gemas in Johore and ending near the east coast at Kota Bahru. This line had little strategic significance for the Japanese and a 200-mile stretch of track between Mentakab in Pahang State and Kuala Krai in Kelantan was ripped up and sent north together with an eighteen-mile stretch of branch-line track which lined Tapah to Telok Anson on the west coast. Thus direct east-west communications in Malaya were severed in the larger interest of Japan's strategic needs. Burma's railway system was similarly cannibalised, though in this case to a much more limited extent, since the arterial lines of Burma were vital to the Japanese in keeping the forward troops supplied and reinforced. The second line of track between Rangoon and Toungoo seems to have been used for this purpose, still leaving one main line running up the important 'railway corridor' to the north.

The Japanese also supplemented their work force with elephants, traditional labourers in the timber industries of Burma and Siam. Delightedly, they pointed out to the prisoners that 'one elephant equals twenty officers,' and of course it was true, for when it came to the business of uprooting stumps or pulling logs, the elephant could usually outperform a prisoner *Kumi*. They worked alongside prisoners in many of the jungle camps as far south as the Wampo group, operating with intelligence and efficiency but usually maltreated and underfed just as the prisoners were. They proved expert at uprooting stubborn tree stumps which they first attacked by kneeling down and pressing with their trunks until the stump was pushed over and its roots loosened, then if an elephant could not prise the stump up and carry it away with tusks and trunk, the beast would wait until a chain had been passed around the stump and then tug it out of the ground. In the same way, they saved the prisoners much labour in dragging felled timber to a collection point for fashioning into bridge members or embankment supports. On stretches of the railroad where there was insufficient timber near at hand the elephants would have the job of wading out into the river and guiding across to the near bank tree trunks which had been felled into the river from the other side. The elephants unfortunately could not actually build bridges and this difficult and dangerous task fell to the lot of the 'white coolies.'

Bridging of one sort or another was required on many parts of the track, whether to cross mighty rivers like the Mae Khlong at Tamarkan or the many smaller streams which ran into the Khwae Noi further up-country. The railway track kept close to the bank of the Khwae Noi whenever there

was flattish land available; but often this was not the case and the trace had to be pushed around mountainsides where bridging was again required in the form of culverts and viaducts over ravines or as track supports when a mountainside was particularly steep and the rock difficult to penetrate. The bridges were remarkable structures in that they were built almost entirely of wood; the addition of bolts, nails or screws was either a refinement which the Japanese considered unnecessary, or else involved the use of scarce materials which they could not provide. For the very large constructions, selected hardwood timber came up by river and was cut to size on the site, usually by laborious hand-sawing, but for smaller works the timber was cut in the nearby jungle, trimmed and dragged to the site. The first stage in most bridging projects was to drive the roughly-shaped timbers into the river bed or ravine bottom to provide a secure base for the superstructure. No mechanical piledrivers were available for this work, so primitive improvised ones were operated by the prisoners themselves, twenty or more men hauling on a rope to raise the weight which when released, crashed onto the upright timber, forcing it down a couple of inches at a time, into the earth or the river bed, whereupon the process was repeated until the Japanese engineers were satisfied. The upper timbers were joined by dovetail or simple butt-joints and held in position by iron staples or wire binding. By such crude means the Japanese would raise bridges that were on occasions several stories high. That they were ever able to take the weight of a laden train was little short of a miracle, but occasionally they could not. Faults and recessions in the cliffs were also bridged by timbers, the supports for which were driven into the rocks below. All these bridging ventures had the added hazard of construction work at considerable

58

height from the ground. Weak and feverish prisoners were often required to labour in most precarious positions and many injuries resulted from Japanese impatience and bad temper at the slow progress of the work. At one or two of the larger cuttings the Japanese had provided a few tubs which ran on light rails for the more rapid disposal of the waste material, and these too brought added dangers to the prisoners since they were moved by hand and when heavily loaded they easily ran out of control on slopes, causing further injuries. In addition to the main railway tasks there was also the job of hacking out the rough road running through the jungle which the Japanese planned to use as an alternative supply route.

In most camps the day's routine began with roll call, followed by breakfast of boiled rice and tea. Then the tools would be collected and the men would trudge off to the line to begin work there at about 8am. The march to work could itself be something of an ordeal as the track progressed. There was a break of about an hour at midday when a meal would be brought out to the prisoners if the camp was nearby, or else they would eat the lunch that they had brought with them, cold cooked rice and a little dried vegetable. The work then continued till about 4pm when they would return, worn out and with perhaps just sufficient time for a wash in the river if the camp was near it, before the evening meal and the second roll-call. No lights were provided by the Japanese, so washing, mending and any other chores would have to be done in the remaining hour of daylight or by the camp fires which the prisoners lit or by the light of a primitive lamp fuelled by palm oil or a mixture of mud and stolen kerosene and flamed with a rag wick. Shortly after dawn the following day the routine would recommence, and so it went on day after day, through 260 miles of jungle, where over 40,000 men from about forty camps, shovelled and dug, picked and carried, sawed trees and built bridges under a fierce tropical sun or in a monsoon downpour, and seldom sustained by a single square meal. In human terms the result was inevitable – it was death for some, critical illness for many and general sickness and debilitation for the remainder.

To appreciate the size of the medical problem with which the European doctors in the jungle camps had to cope, it must first of all be realised that from the point of view of general health the Japanese authorities could scarcely have chosen a worse area in which to concentrate a force of European prisoners. Of the Burma theatre in general the Army Medical Services History has this to say: 'There were very few other theatres on earth in which an army would encounter so many and such violent hazards. In Burma all the dread agents of fell disease and foul death lay in wait.' When General Slim took command of the Fourteenth Army he reckoned the health of his troops to be one of his greatest problems, and pointed out that in 1943 he had 120 men evacuated sick for each one evacuated with wounds. The annual rate for malaria alone was eighty-four per cent per year of the total strength of the army. During the monsoon campaign of 1944 when XXXIII Corps was pursuing a beaten enemy it had a total sick list of 47,000 men, over half the average strength of the Corps, while only 3,200 men became battle casualties. This then was the kind of attrition caused by the climate and the physical conditions of the area on an army of fit men supported by an elaborate medical organisation. It was in precisely these conditions that the European prisoners built the Burma-Siam railway.

In the case of the prisoners, however, their resistance to disease was immeasurably lower than that of the

Above: Labour-intensive bridge building in progress. *Right:* A section of the Wampo bridge showing the cutting which was hacked out of solid rock

fighting units because of their inadequate diet and strenuous work together with primitive living conditions and the almost total absence of the drugs needed to treat their ailments. Rice was their staple food, but it was rice of poor quality, generally broken-grained and much inferior to that which the Japanese consumed. Failures in the Japanese supply system often meant that even the meagre calculated ration did not end up in the prisoners' mess tins; besides which it took the cooks some time, given the primitive utensils with which they did their work, to present the rice in an appetising form. To the basic rice were added minute quantities of protein, either salted fish, buffalo or pork, and a few vegetables such as Chinese cabbage and tapioca root. This, together with small amounts of sugar and tea was all that the allocated ration provided for the prisoners' sustenance.

However, the Japanese did issue

pay to their POWs after a while. It was only a small sum, from which they deducted a proportion for 'bed and board', and further reduced in value by the galloping inflation that prevailed in the occupied territories, but it did provide the means of occasionally supplementing the diet with peanuts, pig oil and duck eggs purchased from the local natives. This was never a regular supply, however, and never available in sufficient quantity. Since most prisoners had existed on this diet since the early days in Changi and Batavia, many were suffering from vitamin deficiency before they ever arrived on the railway, and, once there, the crowded living conditions together with the rudimentary sanitation made the spread of disease unavoidable. Flies

Left: **The interior of an officers' hut by night.** *Above:* **Canteen at which Siamese traders were, for a short time, allowed to trade**

swarmed over the crude latrines, the atap huts and bamboo sleeping platforms were infested with bugs and few prisoners retained mosquito nets to protect them from the insects which invaded the huts in the evenings. The railway work also drained their reserves of energy, making the effort of preserving sanitary conditions in the camps a further tax on their patience and endurance. The inevitable result was that large numbers became seriously ill almost as soon as they arrived in Siam or Burma. At the Beke Taung camp at the Burma end of the line nearly half the force was too sick to work within three weeks of its arrival, and it had already had two deaths from dysentery, while at the Chungkai camp in Siam over thirty per cent of the force was unfit for work by the end of December 1942. This was the scale of the problem with which the doctors were confronted.

Much could have been done for the sick if adequate supplies of drugs and medical equipment had been provided, but they were not. Alternatively the many cases of beri-beri and associated deficiency diseases could easily have been dealt with if a more nutritious diet had been available. Thus the doctors were in the desperate position of being able to diagnose the diseases and sicknesses from which the men were suffering, and of knowing the specifics required for their cure, but they lacked both the drugs and the equipment with which speedy cures could have been effected. The small quantities of dressings and medicines which had been salvaged from Singapore and elsewhere at the time of the capitulation rapidly ran out and the Japanese issued only a minimum of replacements. They did provide a fair amount of quinine, the best-known suppressive for malaria. They had, in fact captured the world's source of supply in Java, forcing the Allied powers into a rapid research programme for alternatives; but even the provision of this drug was irregular and malaria would soon return with its old virulence once a sufferer ceased taking it. Other desperately needed drugs were deliberately withheld from the prisoners, though Red Cross stocks were later discovered in Japanese hands. It is difficult to explain this apparently illogical state of affairs, for denying the drugs to the POWs simply resulted in a further weakening of the labour

the homeland. By 1944 the value of drugs consumed by the civilian population in Japan had declined by seventy per cent, while the difficulty of getting such drugs as were available across the seas to the fighting troops increased each month. This perhaps helps to explain the Japanese attitude to the Red Cross supplies, but it does not excuse the gross inhumanity of some of the POW authorities who not only withheld medicaments from the camp hospitals but also sold them privately for personal profit. One notorious camp commandant would provide much needed idioform only

A typical example of the small bridges built for the Burma-Siam Railway

force, and yet the supplies were not generally issued to Japanese troops whose own medical cover was extremely poor. The answer perhaps lies in the loss of face involved in accepting medical supplies from non-Japanese sources with its inevitable reflection on Japan's status as an advanced nation.

Certainly Japan's own supply of drugs and medicines was rapidly becoming critical as merchant shipping losses progressively isolated

in exchange for prisoners' watches and other valuables, while at another hospital at the south of the line, strips of old rag were used to dress sores while the local Korean guards' football team used new Red Cross bandages as laces for their boots.

The result was that if sick prisoners survived they often did so only because of the brilliant improvisations of the MOs, the careful nursing provided by their comrades and the medical orderlies, and through their own will power. When additional food was available, it would be reserved for the sick, and individual soldiers' private purchases often found their way into the hospital huts for the sustenance of sick friends. The Japanese themselves showed little concern for the sick, either among the prisoners or their own men, many of whom, because their own medical cover was so scanty surreptitiously obtained treatment from the prisoners' doctors. The Japanese doctor officially responsible for all the prisoners of No 3 Group, which included all those in Burma at this time, was a man named Heguchi, who was reputed to have had no formal medical training, and who did little to alleviate the suffering of the hundreds of men in the base hospital at Thanbyuzayat and in the up-country camps. However, the Japanese did favour one prisoner with special attention from one of their own doctors. The man concerned acted as the official interpreter for No 3 Group and his services were obviously considered sufficiently valuable for his life to be preserved. Suffering from appendicitis, he was sent to Moulmein to be operated on by a Japanese surgeon. The operation was performed quite without anaesthetics, the patient being held down throughout its duration by five orderlies.

The general disregard of the sick was accompanied by the belief that sick people ate less, and their rations could accordingly be reduced. All in all it was a situation in which the medical officers might have despaired; instead they responded to the challenge and by their ministrations prevented the labour force from being decimated. Improvisation was thus the watchword for the jungle doctors. Bandages were made from all available strips of cloth; even leaves and raw latex tapped from wild rubber trees were used on occasions; dressings were improvised from the bottoms of mosquito nets, while tin cans and other discarded junk were beaten into bowls and containers. Some medicines were purchased secretly from the natives while others were wheedled from Japanese guards who came for treatment themselves. But despite the best efforts of the doctors the sick queues lengthened. The hospital huts became more crowded as cerebral malaria, dysentery, beri-beri and a host of other complaints took their toll of the labour force and the simple camp cemeteries grew larger as their wooden crosses spread over more and more ground. Some men seemed to die not because they were victims of a killer disease but rather because they finally gave up the struggle to survive; having once taken to their beds they never left them again. Certainly the will to keep going was a vital factor in survival in the jungle camps; there was often nothing else to sustain the sick.

The transformation which disease effected in the appearance of some prisoners was such that friends with whom they had lived and worked for long periods would not recognise them after a couple of months' separation during which they had perhaps contracted dysentery or developed beri-beri. One Australian soldier caught dysentery during the sea passage from Java to Burma and within two months his weight had dropped from its normal ten stone to precisely three stone thirteen pounds. His friends managed to get their hands on a supply of eggs, and stuffing fourteen a day into him, he finally recovered. Beri-beri on the other hand produced a gross swelling of the limbs and face which seemed to mock the inevitable diagnosis of vitamin deficiency. One particularly insidious but common complaint was the jungle ulcer; the tiniest scratch on the skin, particularly from a rough stone or a sharp piece of bamboo, would steadily develop into a growing open ulcer which could eat away at the tissue until it finally exposed the bone. Drug treatment could be remarkably effective for this particular trouble but drugs were very scarce and the only alternative in many cases was frequent curretage of the ulcer;

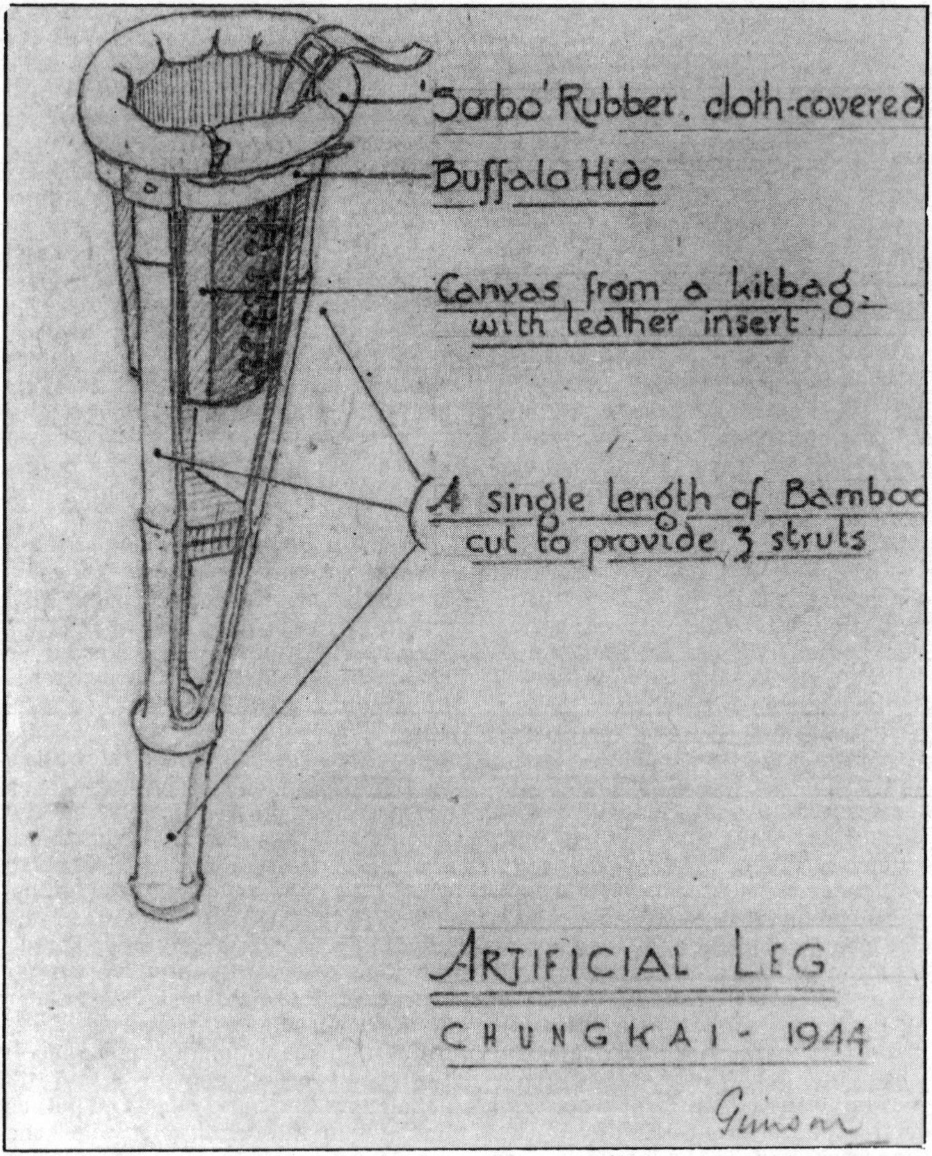

'Sorbo' Rubber, cloth-covered

Buffalo Hide

Canvas from a kitbag, with leather insert

A single length of Bamboo cut to provide 3 struts

ARTIFICIAL LEG

CHUNGKAI - 1944

Gimson

in non-medical terms this meant that the pus had to be scraped out of it with whatever instruments were available, normally a spoon or even a piece of bent tin. It was a grisly and painful business but it did help to save limbs, for if they become grossly infected the only answer was amputation; and even this was frequently and successfully under-taken in the jungle hospitals, in improvised operating theatres, with ordinary implements, using only local anaesthetics, and by the light of oil lamps or fires.

By the end of 1942 the advance parties had been at the railway site for about six months, but the main groups only for a matter of weeks, thus the track had not proceeded

Above: POW-designed beam balance
used for the division of rations and
for weighing hospital patients. *Left:*
An artificial leg; many prisoners lost
legs as a result of injury

very far when the men spent their
first Christmas in captivity. The slow
progress also resulted from the formidable engineering difficulties which
appeared to menace practically every
section of the route from Tamarkan
onwards, the first of them being the
job of bridging the Mae Khlong river
just west of the town. In fact the
Japanese built two bridges over the
river here, the first one constructed
entirely of timber, and the second,
designed for heavier traffic, of con-
crete. For the wooden bridge heavy
square beams of hardwood with
sharpened ends were first floated out
into the river by work parties. The
beams were then tilted upwards and
driven into the river bed by the hand-
operated pile-drivers mounted in a
crude scaffolding. Cross-beams were

connected to these foundation timbers and further sections were added
until the bridge finally reached the
height of the railway track on each
bank. The completed structure was
several hundred yards in length and
about five storeys above the water.
Unremarkable in engineering terms,
the bridge achieved its notoriety for
the primitive manner of its construction by crude labour-intensive
methods. The work required some
prisoners to spend the whole day waist-
deep in the swirling waters, moving
logs into place or holding timbers
while they were secured. Others, in
groups of a dozen or more, operated
the mechanism of the crude pile-
drivers, pulling or releasing the ropes
at the chanted command of the gang
leaders like so many slaves of old.
This bridging work was the task of
men from the camps in the Tamarkan-
Chungkai area, Chungkai being the
headquarters of No 2 Group of prisoners, commanded by Lieutenant
Colonel Yanagida, a comparatively in-

Christmas Morning
anyo 1942.

offensive officer by Japanese standards, but completely dominated by his harsher subordinates. To begin with Chungkai was a busy staging centre, a base for a string of camps, under the aegis of No 2 group, which stretched northwards along the bank of the river. The Japanese finally had six Prisoners Groups on the railway, two based in Burma and four in Siam, though work parties from one Group would, from time to time, be operating in the territory of another. Chungkai became progressively more crowded as more staging parties from the south moved up to it, and groups of sick prisoners from up-country were evacuated to its base hospital. It was also, especially in the dry season, one of the more comfortable camps on the river, particularly since additional food could generally be purchased from the local villagers, though the Chungkai hospital grew depressingly large and overcrowded.

The other major operation in the Chungkai area was the hacking of an enormous cutting through a low hill, most of which was solid rock, while a little further north the infamous Wanlain viaduct was being built. Here a steep cliff blocked the projected path of the track and as there was no possibility of making a detour without immense difficulty, a viaduct was accordingly constructed. It began by running along a shelf hacked out of the cliff face and was then supported on timber trestles bridging gaps and faults in the rock face. The upright timbers stood sixty feet high in some places and were keyed into cracks in the rock lower down. As usual with Japanese bridges, the whole construction was jointed and only fixed with iron staples, and it appeared to hang out over the river which ran far below. Yet despite the difficulties of this section, it was only one short stretch of the whole route and much of the territory beyond it

Church service at 'St Andrew's in the Jungle'

had, as yet, had no more work done on it than the rough clearing needed for the engineers' survey. It was clear that the major transfers of prisoners from Singapore and Java during November and December 1942 had still not provided the Japanese with an adequate labour force for their gigantic undertaking.

However, there were still further drafts to come up from Changi and another group of ex-Java prisoners had yet to make their 'hell-ship' journey to the Burma end of the line. This latter party had started their move very soon after the first Java shiploads had left, but unlike their predecessors, their stay in the Changi compound had lasted nearly three months before they were taken in lorries down to the Singapore dockside and embarked on Japanese cargo boats for their trip to Burma. There were 1,800 men in this group, a mixture of Australians, Dutch and Americans, packed as usual into the cramped holds of the freighters. In mid-January 1943 the little convoy of two cargo boats and a small naval escort had practically reached its destination and was just off Moulmein in the Andaman Sea when two Liberator bombers from bases in India spotted the ships and began to bomb them. They scored three direct hits on the first freighter and its cargo of Japanese soldiers and prisoners were forced to take to the water. Finally the planes sheered off and the second freighter, which was also damaged, circled around picking up the survivors from the first. Four hundred Japanese and about fifty prisoners lost their lives in this attack. This was a harrowing experience for the prisoners before they had even begun their ordeal on the railway, and a grim augury of the hazards of sea passages aboard Japanese ships once the Allies had begun to re-establish their mastery of sea and air in the Indian and Pacific Oceans. The prisoners who ran this gauntlet before arriving in Burma became No 5

Group, working with No 3 Group on the northern end of the project.

The various POW task forces which the Japanese sent from Singapore to destinations throughout the region were known by code letters. The first, 'A' force, had been the 3,000 Australians who worked first on the Burma airfields before being transferred to the railway. By March 1943 the authorities had worked through to the letter 'D'. 'D' Force was a party of 5,000 prisoners, over half of whom were British and the rest Australian, who were bound for the Siam end of

the railway. At this stage the track itself had only been laid as far as Kanchanaburi and 'D' Force was to be employed on embankments and cuttings and other difficult tasks along the line where progress had fallen behind schedule. However, before their departure from Singapore, the men were told by the Japanese that they were being taken to newly-constructed rest camps, in a land where there was an abundance of rice and the natives enjoyed the highest standard of living in Asia. The falsity of this information may not have dawned on 'D' Force during the journey to Singapore railway

A cutting near Tamarkan

Crowded passenger train crosses a flimsy trestle bridge

station, but it soon became clear when they arrived at Bang Pong after the five-day journey on the Nippon 'Golden Arrow' that they were just another part of the multi-national labour force which was to build the strategic railway, or die in the attempt, and the men were soon toiling in the conditions of slavery that the Japanese system demanded. But what came as a rude shock to these new arrivals, and as an added strain to those who were already working, was the new spirit of urgency with which the Japanese were attacking the project. The first job which part of 'D' Force was given was the construction of a huge embankment. It was built

in fifteen days by shifts of prisoners working around the clock, the last shift being kept working for thirty hours, until at last the embankment was completed. 'At its end,' wrote one Australian bombardier, 'we carried dozens of unconscious comrades back to our tents and fell into one of the greatest slumbers of all times.' This was but one example of the frenzied activity which now engulfed the railway labour camps as the Japanese introduced what they called a period of 'speedo working'.

Prelude to the struggle

The need for a more rapid completion of the Burma-Siam railway was dictated by Japan's steadily deteriorating strategic situation. The initial triumphs over Britain, Holland the the United States had come far sooner and far more cheaply than the Japanese had dared to hope. Driven by a conviction of their own invincibility they began to consider expanding their perimeter instead of consolidating it. A major expedition was planned against Midway Island, to draw the American Pacific Fleet into battle and destroy it while, at the southern end of their new Empire, they prepared to capture Port Moresby in Southern New Guinea and Tulagi near Guadalcanal Island, as bases for the further isolation of Australia and New Zealand by the capture of other island groups which lay to the west of these Allied strongholds. But all three operations ended in failure. Forewarned of the impending amphibious assault on Port Moresby, an Allied naval force was assembled and a few days later the first carrier-against-carrier battle in history took place. Tactically, the engagement was a draw, but strategically it was an Allied victory, because the Japanese turned about and abandoned their assault. Later in the year their overland advance on the port proved equally unsuccessful, being halted by Australian troops thirty-two miles from the town. In August 1942 US forces began the reoccupation of Guadalcanal, provoking a violent reaction from the Japanese. Naval battles for the control of the island raged for three full months, while the struggle on land lasted twice as long. Both contests went ultimately against the Japanese, further dissipating their overstretched forces. Much more serious, however, than these defeats in the south, was the disaster which overtook Japan at Midway in June. Here her fleet lost four aircraft carriers and two heavy cruisers in what was perhaps the crucial naval battle of the Pacific War. The United States regained the initiative at sea and now possessed a degree of naval superiority which she was never again to lose, while the Japanese lost the ability to provide mobile air cover for her scattered Pacific garrisons and her weakened fleet.

These setbacks at the eastern end of her Empire inevitably meant that fewer military resources could be deployed at its western extremity to which the growing British strength in north-east India was an increasing menace. India also provided the base from which American aircraft were carrying a steady flow of supplies to Chiang Kai-shek's armies in Yunnan. Even Admiral Yamamoto's highly successful raid into the Indian Ocean in April 1942, with its attacks on Colombo and Trincomalee in Ceylon, had resulted in the loss of a considerable number of veteran naval aviators whose replacement with trained men was proving increasingly difficult. At the end of the year, the British had started an offensive in the Arakan coastal area of Burma, clearly designed to achieve the capture of Akyab with its valuable airfield. This limited assault was later to end in ignominious failure for the British whose Indian Army had been over-expanded in the emergency responses to the rapid succession of military crises with which the British Empire had been confronted. But in the early days of the Arakan offensive it was the Japanese who considered their position to be desperate, as they rapidly switched their 55th Division from central Burma to block the Allied thrust. This renewed British strength on the ground was paralleled by an evident increase in Allied air power.

Initially, the battered remnants of the Burma air force had withdrawn to India whose eastern airfields were quite inadequate as bases for offensive action, even had suitable planes been

Japanese carrier *Shoho*, sunk at the Battle of the Coral Sea

available, which they were not. There were a few Blenheim light bombers, but their range was limited, while the US heavy bombers in India were very much birds of passage, intended for use in China and not under General Wavell's control. Fortunately for the Allies, this period of great weakness in the air coincided with the south-west monsoon when climatic conditions made regular flying a difficult and dangerous undertaking. Nevertheless reconnaissance flights as far south as Rangoon were kept up. During this period the Japanese air force was largely inactive on the Burma front, the principal units of the 5th Air Division having been withdrawn to Malaya and Siam for training and re-equipment, while several air regiments were transferred from the theatre altogether, supporting instead the Japanese armies over mainland China. Meanwhile, the monsoon, which precluded large-scale air activity by the Allies, did give them a breathing space during which they were able to construct new airfields in Assam and bring to combat-readiness the fresh squadrons with which they were at last being reinforced. The result was that when the rains abated in September they were in a much better position to dispute command of the air over Burma with the Japanese, and since the heavily wooded nature of much of the country deprived the bombers of suitable tactical targets, it was on the enemy communications system and the Japanese airfields that they concentrated their attacks. The British bomber squadrons, operating from air strips near Calcutta began a systematic offensive against the railways and the air bases in Burma, conducting their daylight attacks with fighter cover at targets near enough for the range of the escorts, and at night bombing further afield

The doomed *Hiryu*, one of four Japanese carriers lost at Midway

Admiral Yamamoto, C-in-C of the Japanese Fleet

unescorted.

By the end of October 1942 Tenth United States Army Air Force had also been sufficiently reinforced with heavy bombers to undertake major raids on Rangoon, Mandalay and other targets. The Liberators even penetrated as far as Bangkok when, at the end of November, a force of eight of them did a round trip of 2,760 miles for a surprise attack on the Siamese capital's oil refinery and power plant. But it was the Rangoon area that was most persistently and heavily attacked since it was the nodal point of the Japanese supply system and also the one major target that was within operational range of the heavy bombers. These missions were a severe trial for the crews involved; the flying distance was considerable, the weather over the Andaman Sea was very unpredictable and the paucity of information about the movement of Japanese shipping rendered many missions abortive. They were, nevertheless, a grave setback for the

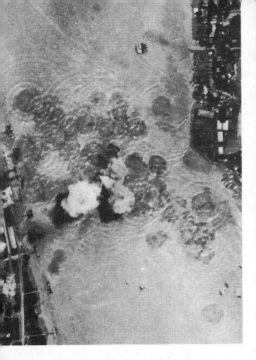

Left: Troops of an Indian brigade in the Arakan. Above: Air attack on Rangoon Harbour. A Japanese vessel explodes in mid-river. Below: The rail junction at Mandalay, an important target for the Allied bombers.
Right: Air attack on the Death Railway

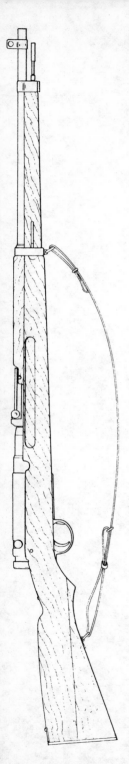

The Japanese Arisaka Type 38 (1905) 6.5mm rifle was one of the two basic rifles used by the Japanese in the Second World War. It was in all ways similar in operation to the Mauser Gewehr 98 except in the safety catch. The type was also fitted with a bolt cover, to keep dirt out of the breech when the bolt was open, but this was usually discarded in the field as it made a considerable amount of noise. The main failing of the weapon was the low power of its cartridge. *Calibre*: 6.5mm. *Operation*: turn bolt. *Length*: 50.2 inches. *Barrel length*: 31.4 inches. *Feed*: 5-round non-detachable staggered-row box magazine. *Weight*: 9.25 lbs. *Muzzle velocity*: 2,400 feet per second

Japanese who still depended upon free movement in the Andaman Sea and control of the facilities at the Rangoon docks in order to operate the 30,000 or 40,000 tons of shipping which needed to make the trip to the port of Burma each week if her forces were to be kept supplied and vital raw materials taken back to Japan. Besides increasing the difficulties of supplying the army in Burma and hindering the movement of raw materials, these Allied air attacks on the Rangoon area also threatened the overtaxed Japanese merchant fleet with further losses which it could ill afford. At the start of the war it had scarcely been able to manage the dual task of military transport and carriage of raw material, and it certainly could not do this work if it sustained any other than minimal losses. However, by the end of 1942 Japan had lost over 240 merchant ships, a gross total of well over 1,000,000 tons. Such losses already outpaced the rate of new building, and the conspicuous growth of Allied air and submarine strength suggested that things might well get worse rather than better. So far as the situation in Burma was concerned, everything seemed to point to the urgent need to dispense with the sea route to Rangoon as a supply line for the Fifteenth Army and to replace it with the overland railway from Bangkok as quickly as possible.

The original completion date for the Burma-Siam railway was November 1943, but the various factors outlined above, including the evident need to reinforce the Burma theatre, increased the pressure to finish the railway by an earlier date. The new target date, announced by Tokyo in February 1943, was August of the same year, for in September the monsoon would be ending and with the skies over Burma clear again the Allied air attacks could be expected to resume with fresh intensity. As the official Japanese government report put it: 'When counterattacks by the British Indian

Army and the bombing of our communications rapidly became fiercer, and the situation in this area considerably worsened after the rainy season of 1942, our sea transportation from Malaya to Burma gradually became more difficult . . . It became evident that if things were left as they were till the end of the next rainy season communications with Burma would be almost entirely interrupted . . . '

The orders therefore went out to Southern Army to speed up the railway work and 'to pay particular attention to the systematic mobilisation of labour.' It was clear that the existing labour force, large though it was, would not be sufficient to complete the project by the revised deadline. The authorities consequently made rapid plans to supplement it by tapping two labour sources, one already heavily drawn upon, but the other as yet only fractionally exploited by the Japanese: the POW compound at Changi, and the native populations of South-East Asia.

The original slogan of 'Asia for the Asians' and the propaganda outlining the benefits which were to accrue to all under the Japanese-sponsored 'Co-prosperity Sphere' had found an immediate response from most of the peoples of the region, with the solitary exception of the overseas Chinese who regarded the despoilers of their homeland with a particular loathing. The attitude of the Chinese did little to blunt the enthusiasm of the majority races who in any case had little love for these industrious immigrants who seemed to dominate so much of the commercial life of their countries. However, the active support of the Malays, Burmese and Javanese for the Japanese project proved to be rather shortlived. For this the forces of Nippon had only themselves to blame, since they displayed a similar harshness towards the bulk of the Asian peoples who came under their military control as they did towards their prisoners of war. When more

sincere and diplomatic civilian administrators and advisors were sent from Tokyo they were made to feel inferior to the military men; and among the military in the occupied areas none were more powerful or more hated than the Japanese military police, the dreaded *Kempei*, a kind of oriental Gestapo who ruled by terrorism and so earned the fear and loathing of those whom Japan wished most urgently to have as friends. The result was that by the folly of their behaviour the military created a situation in which the people of South East Asia never seriously believed that the 'Co-prosperity Sphere' was anything other than latter-day colonial exploitation.

Aside from this shortsightedness on the part of the military, there was also a more deep-seated reason why economic co-operation with Japan gained little support, and this was simply that Japan was unable to make it a viable undertaking. The basic economic fact was that much of South-East Asia depended upon Europe, the United States and India as markets for its primary products and as suppliers of manufactured goods in return. Japan could neither absorb the supply of raw materials which she now had at her disposal, nor could she provide the industrial goods of which her new dependent territories stood in need. She bought and supplied what she could, but the result of her efforts was only increasing economic dislocation in the producer states which she controlled. As the war turned against Japan and as her merchant fleet grew smaller so the economic deterioration of Malaya, Siam, Burma and the Dutch East Indies became more pronounced. Even the commercial traffic within these territories diminished. To take a typical example, Thai merchants were unwilling to continue their traditional rice trade with Malaya when the Malays could pay only in Japanese paper currency whose value dropped alarmingly, causing the

Military currency note issued in Burma

Japanese to react to the worsening financial situation by simply printing more of it. The inevitable result of this economic dislocation was widespread unemployment, burgeoning inflation, a thriving Black Market and shortages of all the basic commodities, particularly rice. None of this worked to Japan's advantage except in so far as it solved the recruitment problem of native labour for the Burma-Siam railway. With the rice ration growing more meagre each day and the prospect of local employment becoming steadily more remote, the promise of good pay, extra rations and decent housing proved a more than adequate inducement to get thousands of Tamil, Chinese and Malay labourers to move north to work on the railway. They travelled in the same steel trucks as had conveyed the prisoners of war, carrying all their belongings with them. Some even took their womenfolk and children, in the fond belief that they would find in Siam similar conditions to those which had existed on the plantations and rubber estates of Malaya. They arrived at the railhead to find that few arrangements had been made for their reception, that their accommodation was wretched and appallingly overcrowded, and that further journeys on foot through the jungle lay ahead of them before they reached their jungle labour camps. One British prisoner recorded his

impressions of the jungle treks of these pathetic coolie forces as follows:

'I pass long lines of these natives walking along the roadway in single file, with their bundles on their heads. They are all numbered but I don't think there is any roll of names kept. As far as we can see, they are divided up into parties of a hundred, and placed in charge of one of their number who acts as an overseer. He is supposed to get his party of one hundred to the next stage of their journey north. What happens if one or two fall out and die by the roadside, as they are doing, I don't quite know. Perhaps they borrow a few from another party.'

In Java the domestic situation was nothing like as bad as in Malaya; the local people consequently proved more resistant to the Japanese blandishments, and the authorities therefore resorted to more brutal trickery to recruit their railway coolies. They started giving free cinema shows in the towns, and after several nights they surrounded and raided all the cinemas, collected all the healthy young male Javanese and press-

Dr Ba Maw, head of the Japanese-sponsored Government of Burma

ganged them on to boats to join their Malayan brethren on the railway. In general, the rations of the native labourers were inferior even to those which the Japanese gave their prisoners of war and their wages, which would have seemed generous in Malaya, were hardly enough to keep them from starvation in Siam. Leaderless, unorganised and undisciplined, many thousands of these native coolies were destined to perish in their camps along the railway, many of them before the expiry of their six month contracts for 'engineering' work in Siam.

In Burma the Japanese were helped in their recruitment of labour for the railway by the government of Dr Ba Maw which the Japanese supported. Prior to the Japanese occupation nearly all the essential labour in Burma was Indian, the native Burmese, like his Malay brother, never having shown himself particularly keen on industrial or manual labour. About half this Indian labour force had been evacuated to India at the time of the invasion leaving the Japanese short of the bodies they needed. In August 1942 Dr Ba Maw issued a declaration outlining a scheme for the organisation of a Central Labour Control Bureau which was to administer a labour corps. Later he announced a plan for the organisation of the whole people for the purposes of the war, reconstruction and development. The national effort was to be mobilised in four 'armies', one of which, 'The Sweat Army', was the successor to his

others took bribes to excuse men from service, and unscrupulous doctors sold certificates of physical unfitness. Nevertheless recruits did come forward, perhaps as a result of the growing unemployment in agriculture and the various inducements held out by the Japanese, including a prize for the best song written for the Sweat Army. Significantly, entries were to be addressed to the Japanese Military Propaganda Department. There was also to be a Labourers' Welfare Union for the railroad force, and all sorts of amenities, but few of

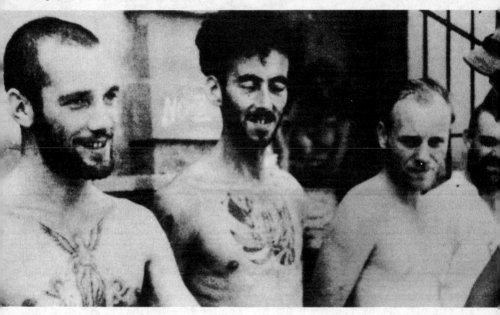

Tattooed British prisoners attract their captors' attention

earlier announced labour corps. The principal task of the Sweat Army was to help in the building of the Burma-Siam railway, and the road which was being developed alongside it. Service in the Sweat Army practically amounted to conscription since local headmen were ordered by their superiors, the Township Officers, to fill specific quotas for the force. One headman hid all his relatives and forced his enemies to join, while

these ever materialised. A second labour force, the *Heiho Tat*, was enlisted directly by the Japanese and formed a general coolie or pioneer force. There is little reason to believe that the Japanese provision for this Burmese element of their railway task force was much better than for the rest; food was poor, medical attention lacking and camp conditions generally bad. Desertion was therefore common and comparatively easy for the Burmese working in his homeland.

The second source of manpower for

the impending hectic phase of railway construction was the still considerable number of prisoners of war concentrated at Changi in Singapore. There were already about 50,000 Allied prisoners along the railway trace but a further 16,000 remained at Changi from whom the Japanese now proposed to select two forces for some of the most gruelling work. These were known henceforth as 'F' and 'H' forces, and they were despatched from Singapore to their jungle destinations in April and May 1943 respectively. The information which the Japanese gave to these unfortunate parties was evidence of the pointless duplicity of many of their announcements to prisoners. Some were told simply that they were going up-country, and nothing more; others that they were going to undertake purely administrative work in the already excellently improved camps in Siam where food and health were good. At least one party was told at a briefing in Singapore station that they would have to build and administer a huge camp in the hills near the Burma border, where there was a plateau 6,000 feet high, and that there they would receive all the railway workers who would come for rest and recuperation when the line was completed. The absence of firm information led inevitably to the spread of rumours, one of which contained the story that the destination of 'F' and 'H' Groups was a series of Red Cross camps in the Malayan hills, where there would be good food, adequate medicines and even some amenities. Some prisoners had secret doubts but just as many regarded the move from Changi as a change for the better. It was thus with shock and despair that these men greeted their arrival at Ban Pong, or in some cases at Kanchanaburi further up the line. Here, they began the series of forced marches that were to take them to the jungle camps deep in the interior of the country and, for some parties, further

than any of the previous labour forces had ever penetrated.

To understand the plight of 'F' and 'H' forces one has to remember that they had now been captives of the Japanese for well over a year, existing in Changi on a diet that was quite insufficient and unsuitable for European stomachs, and that many of them had undertaken no strenuous activity for many months. Some had avoided the earlier work parties because they were too old or too sick for labouring jobs, or because they had not recovered from wounds dating from the Malayan campaign or from the brief struggle for Singapore. They were totally without the rough training for the jungle ordeal that the earlier drafts had had in the first stage of the railway work, and they were lacking in experience in the building of atap huts, living in tents and generally looking after themselves in primitive conditions and with no help from the Japanese. It had been decreed by the railway authorities that 'F' Force was to be 7,000 strong, and it mattered little to the Japanese that there were not, at the time, 7,000 fit men at Changi. There were consequently about 1,000 unfit British prisoners and more than a hundred sick Australians in the force that began to leave Singapore on 16th April in a succession of thirteen trains. The majority also tried to take too much kit with them; they were burdened with bulging packs, bed rolls and even suitcases and officers' valises. Some even attempted to take pianos with them to their up-country sanatoria. Needless to say, these were unceremoniously dumped at Ban Pong when the true nature of their journey became apparent, for it was from this rail terminus that many of the parties began their marches, often by night, of stages up to sixteen miles at a time, that were to take them 180 miles into the interior.

They were also unprepared for the treatment meted out to them by the

Japanese, for at Changi the prisoners within the compound had few direct dealings with their masters, and only those who had worked in outside labour gangs had much inkling of the kind of treatment which they were to receive. Men who fell out during the marches either because of the onset of fever, disease, or through sheer exhaustion were beaten and kicked till they staggered to their feet and rejoined the trudging columns. Those who were too weak to stir were collected in trucks and taken to rejoin their party. If they were too ill to be moved, they were left at a nearby camp to finish their march with one of the groups following behind. What made the situation even worse was that 'F' Force was bound for the remotest part of the jungle trace. In the first section of their march they spent their rest periods in camps already constructed and where arrangements for feeding them had sometimes been made in advance, but eventually their trek took them past all the camps previously occupied in Siam and consequently those who could still move about had to labour inexpertly to erect bamboo shelters against the impending rains, while their comrades, shattered by privation and disease, began to die around them. It was useless to warn staggering, heat-crazed men about the dangers of drinking unboiled water, and so, without adequate food, their resistance already lowered by fourteen months of captivity, they went down like flies with fever and dysentery. All this before their work on the railway had even started.

'H' Force began its life in late April 1943 in response to a request from the Railway Corps for a further 3,270 men to work on the middle reaches of the trace where progress had been slow. Similar blandishments attended its recruitment as had been used with 'F' Force, and like its predecessor it too contained a high proportion of unfit men. The Force began to leave Singapore by rail on 5th May and started its

jungle marches five days later. By the middle of the month the first parties were arriving at their destinations with the prisoners' in the last stages of exhaustion, limping, staggering and swaying like drunken men. If 'H' Force's approach march was shorter than that of its predecessor, its work on the railway was just as gruelling, for the thirteen-mile stretch of territory between Tonchan and Hintok in which it was to operate, was noted for its difficulty.

While the last Singapore groups were beginning their marches to the railway camps, the existing labour forces were also being reorganised for the next phase. The base camps were left to the growing numbers of sick while the fitter men moved on to new areas. The headquarters of No 2 Group was switched from its relatively pleasant location at Chungkai to Takanum at the 206 kilometre mark, deep in the jungle belt yet in a strangely well-developed area, for

Tarsau Camp, in thickening jungle

near it lay a small Thai town which acted as a sort of collection centre and administrative headquarters for the wolfram mines nearby, to which it was connected by an asphalt road. No 4 Group headquarters moved to Tarsau, the gateway to the jungle proper, which became a kind of half-way house on the journey to camps further north, and its area of responsibility covered a stretch of track lying principally to the north of it, as far as the Dutch camp of Rin Tin which had acquired an unenviable reputation for sickness and disease. Between these two places the route covered a particularly difficult mountain stretch where limestone ledges were blasted out of the hillside to take the line and apparently flimsy wooden bridges were built over precipices a hundred feet deep; for ten kilometres at a stretch the railway line in this area would have to run through a series of precariously blasted cuttings, over steep embankments and across culvert bridges wedged high in the hills.

But one had to travel past all the No 4 Group camps, and through those of No 2 Group beyond to reach the area where 'F' Force was based in a series of makeshift encampments between Kon Kuta and the Burma frontier at the Three Pagodas Pass. These camps achieved the notoriety of having the highest death rate of the whole railway. Across the border in Burma No 3 and No 5 Groups were now disposed along the more remote stretches of the trace which spanned the 113 kilometres between Than-byuzayat and the frontier with Siam. The railway was now taking traffic at both ends and trains were running for some distance into the interior, pulled by ancient engines sent from Java and Malaya and fired by wood fuel instead of the coal on which they had been designed to operate.

'Speedo'

This then was the situation in May 1943 when the Japanese, having amassed a labour force of 61,000 Allied prisoners and over a quarter of a million Asian workers, set about 'hastening' the construction of the railway. The whole gigantic organisation was now subjected to the intense pressure of the 'speedo' policy which started as the first sharp tropical showers heralded the coming of the monsoon and which was to continue until the last rail was laid. For the prisoners the 'speedo' period was quite simply a desperate struggle for survival with all the odds stacked against them. The monsoon produced infinitely more difficult working conditions and brought fresh outbreaks of disease with it, while at the same time it washed away bridges and turned roads into streams, at times completely severing the communication routes by which the Japanese brought food supplies to the camps. None of these difficulties, however, affected the single-minded determination of the Siam garrison forces to compel their prisoners to complete the railway on time. Their policy towards the sick was crudely laid bare by the commander of No 5 Group in Burma who declared: 'Any sick man who staggers to the line to lay one sleeper will not have died in vain,' while another officer exposed the nature of the prisoners' dilemma with the words, 'You do not understand us. We will build this railway if necessary over the bones of the POWs,' for at the time it seemed to many that it was impossible both to complete the work and yet to survive to see it ended. Without the monsoon the task would have been imposing enough, with it the ordeal was frigh-

Chungkai camp in 1944

Boot repairing by convalescent prisoners

tening to consider.

In 1943 the monsoon proper broke on 22nd May and for the next sixteen days the driving rain lashed the railway trace almost without pause. The Khwae Noi rose in flood and swamped several of the jungle camps completely, every unmade road and jungle track became a watercourse and a layer of thick glutinous mud lay on the surface of even the higher camps. The rain found holes in the best constructed atap huts and it poured through the desperately inadequate tents which were all that some of the workers had for housing. Drainage in many of the camps was impossible and water lay in great stagnant pools. The men were never dry; after a rain-soaked day's work on the line they would return to a meal of watery rice which the rain further diluted as it was being eaten, and then they would retire, saturated, muddy and exhausted to a wet bamboo bed or a sodden canvas one in a hut that leaked or a tent that failed to keep out the rain but turned it instead into a fine penetrating spray. The dawn would bring another round of grinding work and saturation. So difficult did it become to keep the up-country camps supplied with food that the more isolated of them had to be abandoned when the monsoon reached its height, while in others food stocks fell perilously low. Moreover, the Thai canteen barges which regularly moved up-river to sell food to the prisoners during the dry season, now

Thai barge and water fatigue party on the Khwae Noi

southern regions, but from May 1943 onwards there developed on the railway a crescendo of violence designed to spur the workers on to greater efforts, but which in fact often only weakened them further, rendering them even less able to meet the fearsome work tasks which their captives laid down. Commanding officers were beaten for trying to protect their men from some of the grosser injustices of their captivity; medical officers were beaten for trying to prevent sick men from being ordered out with the working parties, whose *hanchos* and *kumichos* were also assaulted for a variety of shortcomings, which were mostly designed to save the men from extra or unnecessary labour, like conniving at an overlong tea-break or permitting a weak prisoner to take an unauthorised rest, while the men themselves were continually being thrashed for slowness at a particular task or even for failing to comprehend instructions screamed at them in Japanese. At such times the enraged guards would strike out with their hands or boots or with whatever implements were within reach; many kept bamboo sticks specifically for the purpose, others would lay about the men with pick handles or the flat of a sword. Prisoners were frequently knocked senseless, some had bones broken, while at times a beating would be followed by a specific punishment, such as holding a rock above the head for hours on end, or standing to attention all day outside the camp guard room. The man who could hold up the rock no longer or who tottered weakly from his position of attention would receive a fresh beating for disobedience. The physical torment of prisoners was not just something in which ill-disciplined guards indulged when their superiors were not around, it was part of a disciplinary system in which the engineers and Japanese

made the journey much less frequently. Some camps went for weeks without the chance of supplementing their diet with an occasional duck egg purchased from the traders. All in all, so far as the health of the prisoners, and the general working conditions on the railway were concerned, the Japanese could hardly have chosen a worse time for a speeding-up of the project.

Furthermore, the new 'speedo' policy exposed in the most brutal way possible the radical difference between the Japanese and the Allies in their respective treatment of prisoners of war. The beating of prisoners had been a feature of the Japanese system ever since the first working parties had been organised in the camps in the

officers of the POW administration fully participated; indeed some of the worst beatings were handed out by the officers themselves. It was, however, a practice which did little to speed up the building of the railway.

During the monsoon 'speedo' the workers took breakfast in the dark and were frequently already at work before it was properly light. The working day became so extended that some groups did not see their camp again until nightfall. On stretches of the track where the work was particularly difficult or had fallen behind schedule, round-the-clock shift-working was introduced, the trace being lit up with carbide lamps and bonfires. During this period there was seldom such a thing as a standard length of time for a shift; there are examples of them lasting twenty-four and even on one occasion thirty-six hours. Camp administrative staffs were cut to the bare minimum so that more of their number could join the labour gangs. This was doubly unfortunate since these prisoners had generally got their camp jobs because they were 'light sick' in any case, and also because their jobs of cooking, cutting firewood, digging latrines and drawing water were basic to the existence of the whole camp and could not possibly have been undertaken by the working parties after an overlong day on the line. Inevitably standards of camp administration fell, and at the very time when the sick-rate was reaching alarmingly high figures, putting an immense and ever-increasing strain on the medical officers.

Mention has already been made of the 'base hospitals' which were set up by the various prisoner groups at their principal camps, though the impressive name of these improvised medical organisations merely reflected the distressing size of the problem confronting them, rather than any abundance of drugs or equipment for the Japanese

Makeshift cookhouse for 150 convalescent prisoners

provided little of either. The hospitals were usually staffed by several medical officers drawn from the ranks of the prisoners, but they had little extra to offer except a broader range of expertise; their only advantage came from their location nearer to established supply routes, and in certain cases they were supervised by more senior and slightly more co-operative Japanese officers. Their larger staffs and their distance from the areas of the most frenzied railway activity also served to protect their patients from the singleminded demands for a specified size of labour gang irrespective of the sickness of individual members of it, which was a continual harrassment for the medical officers at the jungle camps.

But what they gained in this respect, the base hospitals lost in overcrowding, as the up-country camps tried to evacuate to them as many sick men as possible before the advent of the worst monsoon conditions. At Thanbyuzayat the base hospital had been extremely overcrowded long before the monsoon had started and it was only after repeated representations that the Japanese agreed to the building of some new huts for the sick who were coming down from the jungle in greater numbers each week. By June 1943 this hospital had 3,000 patients crowded into fourteen long huts, indistinguishable from the Japanese storehouses and barracks which surrounded them, and located close to the railway sidings and accumulated stocks of sleepers and other railway materials. In May, the Allied bombers had struck at Moulmein, causing a mass exodus of the frightened inhabitants into Siam, and the following month the air forces extended their activities to Thanbyuzayat itself. A raid on 12th June killed nine prisoners and wounded eight others, while three days later seventeen were killed and many more injured when a second flight of Liberators again attacked what they took to be a perfectly legitimate military target. The Japanese finally agreed to move the hospital away from this obvious bombing objective, but since the journey to a safer area had to be made on foot by all but the totally immobile patients, and because the camps to which they were sent were ill-prepared to receive them, the result was only an increase in the death rate and a worsening of the condition of the remaining sick, some of whom were forced to march the thirty kilometres to Retpu where a main camp hospital had been set up. It was small consolation to know that Thanbyuzayat was heavily bombed on five separate occasions during June shortly after the patients had been moved.

The camp hospitals in the jungle had yet to suffer from the visitations of the bombers, indeed many of them never did, but their problems were already daunting enough, particularly for the single medical officer who was often the only qualified staff member they had, though in some camps there were also trained medical orderlies. From May until October 1943 the camp MOs were under the most intense strain, for as the size of the labour force dwindled the Japanese demanded that more sick men should be turned out to work. The purely medical aspect of their work was a sufficiently imposing task for the jungle doctors, who were not, of course, immune from disease themselves, but during the 'speedo' period they had each day to argue with the camp authorities to dismiss the worst sick from the morning work parade. This was often an unavailing additional task: the Japanese always insisted on the provision of a labour party of a certain number of men despite the daily decrease in those who could be called fit. Thus the doctors would be faced with agonising choices, trying to decide which sick men could get through a day's work on the railway. But even this was better than letting the guards choose the men themselves, for in their ignorance they would

Above: Bombing destroys a main-line bridge and damages the by-pass bridge
Below: The two Tamarkan bridges over the Mae Khlong under attack

spare a man with bandages covering his jungle sores from any labour, but choose instead a prisoner whose limbs, swollen with beri-beri, gave an appearance of health, at least to the untutored eye of the Japanese or Korean guards. Patients with dysentery suffered similarly, even the Japanese doctor, appointed to oversee the medical arrangements for the entire Burma section of the labour force either refused to admit, or had not the knowledge to realise, that amoebic dysentery was rife among the prisoners; he called it 'hill diarrhoea.'

Against this background the jungle doctors laboured to keep their comrades alive. Medical specialists from the finest teaching hospitals in the world, conscripted for the war, worked alongside newly-qualified doctors, passing on information about improvised equipment, trying out fresh jungle sources of protein suggested by prisoner dieticians and pooling the knowledge of experts in tropical diseases with the skill of brilliant surgeons. They carried out many operations, working often in the open, their efforts ranging from a relatively simple appendectomy to the major amputation of a leg. Spinal injection of a local anaesthetic was usually the most that could be given to surgical cases, amputees being well aware of what was going on, though

feeling no pain, and separated from the working surgeon by a bamboo screen placed across the body. A remarkable number of prisoners who underwent amputations did well, and when recovered gained weight and remained in good health. Many were saved by primitive blood transfusions, for which donor and patient lay on adjacent platforms. The blood would be taken from the donor by a fine bamboo cannula placed in a vein in his arm and led through tubes improvised from hollow bamboo and the tubing from stethoscopes to a bamboo cup, where the fibrin would be removed by brisk stirring for a few minutes with a whisk. From there the blood

would pass to the patient via a bottle and another section of improvised tubing and cannula. For some tropical diseases no improvised treatment was possible and since the drugs for their cure were not available, the patients died in their hundreds. The sufferers from deficiency diseases also added to the number of dead; among those who survived there were some who went blind for lack of vitamins.

The medical situation in the railway camps was already desperate when in May 1943 cholera struck. In the century since it had first reached Europe this acutely infectious disease had been regarded with a particular horror, largely on account of the speed with which it can spread and kill. The source of the scourge lay in a region of India near Calcutta, in epidemic terms on the very doorstep of the Burma-Siam railway, and being principally water-borne, its spread during the monsoon was inevitable. It appeared to strike first at the up-country Burma camps, but its progress to camps in Siam was rapid. In normal circumstances it is not difficult to halt the march of cholera, by killing the bacteria before they are taken into the system, by boiling all drinking water, cooking food well and taking steps to prevent its subsequent contamination and by plunging all eating utensils in boiling water; but such measures were not easy to implement given the conditions of the camps, and their institution provided further hardships for the prisoners. Bathing in the Khwae Noi and the smaller streams was prohibited, water for washing was restricted and the small supplies of permanganate of potash that were available were used to disinfect cooking and food-serving implements. However, the internal disciplinary system of the camps was already subject to intense strain and it was consequently not surprising that the occasional man, thirst-crazed

97

One end of the skin wards at Chungkai hospital

and perhaps half-delirious from an attack of malaria, should take a drink from a jungle stream and thus start another cholera outbreak, whose progress in each patient was a horrible spectacle. Cholera is essentially a wasting disease in which the body loses its liquid and becomes dehydrated. The shrinking of the soft tissues can be seen within a few minutes and the patient, shrivelled and monkey-like, mercifully succumbs in a few days or even hours. The camp hospitals managed to save a proportion of even their cholera patients, who were kept strictly isolated in separate huts. Proper treatment required large quantities of saline solution but there was never sufficient provided, and the supply of serum which the Japanese got to the camps often came too late and in quantities too small for the protection of all the prisoners. The parties of 'F' and 'H' forces who went straight from Singapore to the remoter jungle camps were hit particularly heavily by disease; they were ill-prepared as it was for their railway slavery and the addition of cholera to their already desperate conditions brought a very high death rate. The Japanese regarded the outbreak as particularly serious and some of them took to wearing gauze masks during the epidemic and had their areas fenced off from the prisoners' compounds which they did not enter until the disease had run its course. They also ordered that the bodies of those who had died from cholera

Right: A night orderly on duty in a hospital hut. *Below:* The cemetery at Chungkai POW camp

should be burnt, and evening processions to the funeral pyres became common occurrences. These were the times of greatest tribulation and strain for the doctors; at night they would be in the cholera compound injecting saline to stimulate the stricken men who were at other times attended by the orderlies who had volunteered to nurse them, cut off from the sight and sound of their fellows amid the dead and dying. In the early morning they would return to the main camps and after being thoroughly disinfected the daily argument with the guards would begin over the drafting of sick men to the working parties, after which they would turn to the treatment of the other sick.

The worst sufferers of all in the monsoon of 1943 were the coolie forces of Asian peasants. They had no trained leaders to organise them and their ideas of hygiene were extremely primitive. Consequently, dysentery and cholera swept through their ranks like a forest fire, spread by the swarms of flies which infested their sordid camps, and by the absence of any precautions such as the boiling of water and the covering of food. The medical situation rapidly became so chaotic that the Japanese were forced, in an effort to improve the situation, to organise two drafts of medical personnel from among the POWs still at Changi. The forty-five doctors and several hundred orderlies who were sent up to the railway found the task quite beyond them; they were too few, too late and, as always, ill-equipped. One Australian doctor, for example, not knowing a word of their language, was the only medical officer for about 3,000 Asiatics, while at a Tamil 'base hospital' near Takanum two young British doctors found themselves in charge of over 1,000 sick Indians suffering from a wide variety of ailments; their only drug was a limited quantity of potassium permanganate and they were quite without anaesthetics or surgical instruments. The condition of the camps of the Asian workers was made worse by their resigned and fatalistic attitude; sick men were left where they fell at the side of the jungle tracks and many cholera sufferers were merely removed from their huts and left to die at the jungle fringe or slung straight into the river. So serious a problem did these foetid camps become that the Japanese were compelled to organise parties of their European prisoners to clean them up and dispose of the corpses. One British officer was beaten up for refusing to 'finish off' a Tamil dying of cholera, a duty which a Japanese guard performed without hesitation with the flat of a spade. The corpses were heaped into communal graves or else burned on bonfires. Of all the fatigues which the Japanese had their prisoners perform on the Burma-Siam railway, this task was perhaps the most macabre and dehumanising.

Among all the camps in which the European prisoners lived, those of 'F' Force, in the remote Nikki area, were worst hit by sickness and disease. Many parties ran straight into the cholera epidemic as soon as they arrived after their gruelling marches, and some had a seventy-five per cent sickness rate in the first month. At the end of June the Japanese at last decided to establish a base hospital for 1,700 of the worst sick in the force, at Tanbaya across the Burma border, but conditions worsened nevertheless and in four months 750 of the patients at Tanbaya died. By August two-thirds of the 'F' Force men were hospitalised and the Japanese, desperate for labourers, were forcing the stretcher cases to be carried out onto the railway where they broke up stones as ballast for the track. But 'F' Force was not the only one to suffer particularly badly during the monsoon 'speedo'; 'H' Force was similarly hard hit, and across the border in Burma No 5 Group was enduring the tyranny of a particularly unpleasant Japanese commander, Captain Mizdani, who penalised the sick men of his labour force by not allowing them

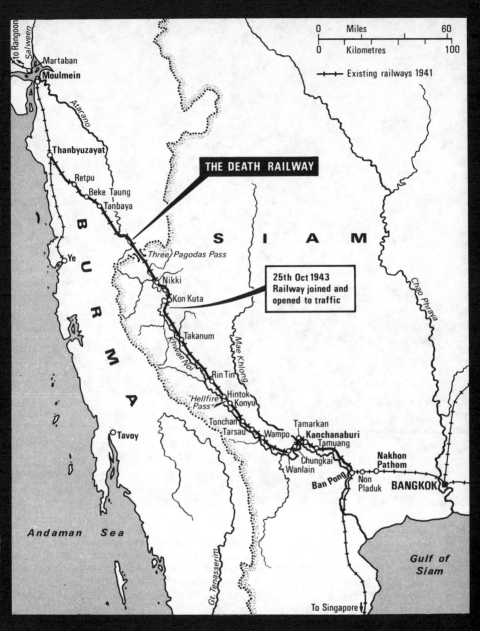

The Burma-Siam Railway, showing the principal POW labour camps

The 'Pack of Cards' bridge at Hintok

to send home the simple POW letter card which had been issued to all other prisoners. There were also, on both sides of the border, groups of prisoners organised as mobile labour gangs which moved up and down the track, travelling by river generally, to carry out small construction jobs or to aid other work parties. They would usually be attached to a nearby camp, but this administrative connection was tenuous in the extreme and they were invariably short of supplies and often without medical cover. These groups were always on the move, never staying in one place long enough for the living conditions to be made bearable and frequently both the prisoners and their Japanese and Korean guards lacked the bare necessities of life. Many died and more besides were hospital cases, utterly worn out by the work and the inadequate food.

In view of the desperate conditions of the railway camps it is remarkable that so few of the prisoners of war succumbed to mental disorders; the bulk of them remained sane and relatively disciplined throughout, some preserving a quick sense of humour even at the height of their adversity. The strain of the daily struggle for existence did tend to peel away the larger loyalties, but the men preserved their individual friendships and units still operated as cohesive forces even when their members became morose and irritable and quarrels arose. The apparent hopelessness of the situation did however induce quite a few men to attempt escape despite the daunting obstacles in the way of success, the distance to the nearest friendly forces and the formidable character of the intervening territory. One early bid was made by a group of eight Australians from the advance party which had operated at Tavoy in Burma. They were quickly recaptured by the Japanese and their Burmese agents and were shot soon afterwards, being forced to kneel beside a burial pit dug by their fellow prisoners, and into which their bodies were unceremoniously bundled. A similar fate befell a party of three Dutch escapees at Thanbyuzayat, while further south at Tamarkan two British officers were at large for three weeks in the jungle before they were recaptured and brought back to camp where, after a short questioning, they were bayoneted. There are no records of successful escapes by Europeans POWs from the railway camps and most attempts ended in execution though there were cases of recaptured prisoners being sent off to a civilian jail and a fate which is not recorded.

Ultimately even the single-minded Japanese had to admit that they could not meet the target date for the all-important railway. As their official report put it, ' . . . as however, the rainy season of 1943 set in earlier than usual the conditions in the jungle worsened from April onwards and the victims of the work gradually increased. Confronted with these bad conditions, Imperial General Headquarters at last postponed the target date for completion of the railway for

two months.' The decision did not in fact amount to a change of policy, the work was already behind schedule and the same pressure was exerted on the labour force until the last length of rail was laid. Even in the better organised camps the problems for the prisoners were enormous. Some camps lay a considerable distance from the stretch of railway on which the men were working and they consequently had a march of as much as eight miles back to camp at the end of their working day. Since this was often after dark and undertaken by men who were both sick and exhausted, individuals would inevitably drop out and on occasions it would be midnight before search parties of their comrades could find them all and carry them back to their huts. In the group of camps around Konyu the main task was the hacking of a huge cutting through solid rock; this stretch became known as 'Hellfire Pass' and one officer who had access to medical records and reports estimated at the time that sixty-eight men were beaten to death in the cutting by Japanese attempting to 'hasten' the work. Further north at Hintok a huge bridge was being built and here the engineers' skill in improvisation did not prevent lengthy delays; for the bridge, almost a quarter of a mile long and eighty feet high when finally erected, collapsed three times during its construction. The bridge also claimed the lives of thirty-one men in falls from it, while nearly as many again were reported to have died as a result of beatings they received while working on it. Nevertheless, the long working hours and slave-driving of the labour force ultimately produced the desired result. Throughout October the rail-laying parties had slowly been drawing together and towards the end of the month the last line was laid with great ceremony some miles south of the Three Pagodas Pass and on 25th of the same month the railway was open to traffic.

Reorganisation

That the completed railway was something of a flimsy structure is perhaps not surprising, given the speed with which it was built and the almost total lack of modern engineering equipment for the construction of some of its more difficult stretches. Journeys on it proved to be rather slow and at times hair-raising experiences and accidents were frequent. In calculating some of the gradients the Japanese engineers had obviously expected too much from the engines to be used. In the main, these were locomotives taken from the Javanese and Malayan railway and the odd diesel engine from Thailand. The steam engines were wood-fired and were frequently unable to develop sufficient power to take them up the steep inclines. One prisoner records that a train in which he was travelling had to stop three times owing to the steepness of the gradient, which proved beyond the capacity of the two engines which were operating on wood fuel. As it was, most of the engines were rather ancient, one of them sporting the admission: 'Made in Doncaster AD 1898'. There were also stretches where the unevenness of the track caused the engine to leave the rails if the driver made any attempt to travel at a reasonable speed. In other sections the sleepers were laid askew and not at right angles to the rails they supported, and this, coupled with a certain amount of subsidence of the ballast during the monsoon rains, sufficed to make stretches of otherwise level track as conducive to accidents as some of the more obviously perilous runs. Another problem was the explosive growth of tropical vegetation which rapidly advanced to reclaim the land taken from it, making track maintenance a continual necessity.

Most prisoners had the doubtful pleasure of making journeys along the railway which so many of their fellows had died constructing, and some have recorded that they were more fearful for their survival at such moments than they were at any other time during their incarceration, for numbers of derailed trucks littered the sides of embankments or lay smashed like matchwood at the bottom of ravines and the bridges creaked and groaned as they took the weight of loaded trains. This fear was intensified by the recollection of the many efforts they had made to sabotage the project. For example, working parties who were building bridges had carefully gathered queens of the white ant, a large jungle termite, and buried them beside the foundation timbers in the hope that they would attract the rest of the swarm and eat away at the supports which were not protected in any way either above or below the ground. Others had sawn through support bolts when the attention of the guards had been diverted, or unscrewed nuts that had already been 'passed' by an inspection of Japanese engineers. On some stretches of the embankment tree trunks had been inserted and then lightly covered with soil, while elsewhere ballast had been deliberately laid unevenly. Nevertheless, the railway was at last working, and the Japanese authorities declared a holiday to celebrate its completion and ordered special memorial services for those who had died in building it.

The Japanese themselves fêted their great engineering achievement with

Japanese guard hut and look-out post at Chungkai

106

as much style as the local circumstances would allow. The last rail to be laid was a special copper one, secured, it is said, with a gilded spike, which was apparently stolen by an Australian prisoner shortly afterwards. The opening ceremony itself was attended by the Japanese senior officers of the railway administration and local dignitaries, who made their way up to the junction point in a special train of open trucks roofed with atap which the POWs christened the 'flying kampong.' Parties of the fittest prisoners were collected from nearby camps and taken up to the spot where the lines joined just south of Kon Kuta to be photographed for the benefit of the readers of the local Japanese propaganda newsheets. The celebration for the garrison troops also included a visit by a Japanese 'brothel train', the soldiers preparing themselves for the occasion by putting on clean uniforms, shining their boots and visiting the prisoners' camp barbers to have their wispy chins shaved and their eyebrows trimmed. In at least one camp the girls gave cigarettes and money to prisoners

by this time was a battered hat and a 'Jap happy', a kind of primitive loincloth.

The memorial services were conducted with great feeling and sincerity by the prisoners and took place at the jungle cemeteries which were dotted along the 260 miles of railway between Ban Pong and Thanbyuzayat. In some camps the ceremony was limited to a few hymns and prayers, in others it was preceded by a formal parade organised in as traditional a way as the emaciated POWs could manage, with the various regiments and corps lining up in order of precedence, though by this stage in the railway tribulations some of the sub-units which marched forward onto their markers were pitifully small. At the HQ Camp of No 2 Group at Takanum there was a representative squad from practically every branch of the British army. At many camps the Japanese insisted on playing an official role in the memorial services. their men decked out in their best dark green uniforms and the officers wearing their long, decorative swords. Some of the Japanese commanders also joined in the ceremony of laying wreaths of jungle flowers on the graves of the men whose deaths were a direct result of Japanese policy and their treatment of the railway prisoners. At Takanum the Group Commander, Colonel Yanagida, delivered a funeral oration at the grave of a British officer.

Across the border in Burma similar ceremonies took place, two days in November being selected for the official celebration of the railway's completion. Here too, all the camps held memorial services, the Japanese once again insisting on laying wreaths on special wooden crosses, erected for the occasion in the middle of the camp cemeteries. In the camps of No 3 Group in Burma the assembled prisoners had read out to them a

whom they saw working nearby. For their particular contribution to the project the prisoners were given what was called a 'Tojo present' of tinned fish. In addition each man in No 2 Group who had not been sick and off work during the building of the line was given an extra present of one Thai tickal, a sum which the current inflation was rapidly making valueless. In some camps there was also a special issue of rubber boots and cheap cotton shorts. The latter did not last long but were a boon to the many prisoners whose sole item of clcthing

A church hut built at Chungkai camp

VICTORY NEWS

ALLIES MASS FOR THE KILL !

PATROLS STAB INTO GERMANY AS HUGE ARMIES PREPARE THEIR FINAL ASSAULT

HUGE Allied armies stand poised for the death-blow about to be delivered to Germany. Patrols are already piercing the German defences—on German soil. Soviet soldiers stand in East Prussia. The steel encirclement of Germany is complete.

Hitler is pulling in his battered armies. From Finland to the Balkans German divisions are trying to withdraw to the tottering Fatherland.

British and American armies on the West Front and Russians in the East are massing

BATTERED JAPS TRY TO REORGANISE

REMNANTS of the Japanese 15 and 31 Divisions

Blackout Ends

Britain's blackout, five years old and cause of many a bruised body, is relaxed from September 17.

This shows the world that Germany's Luftwaffe is no longer considered a menace to our homes.

When double summertime ends ordinary peacetime curtains can be used when the lights are on.

Streets will be brighter and vehicles will have more lighting.

NEW AIR BLOWS

IN PACIFIC

THE Bonin Islands, in Japan's inner defence ring only 600 miles from the Japanese mainland, have been attacked from the air for three days running and bombarded from the sea for two successive days. These raids began on August 30.

The Japanese lost 85 planes destroyed or damaged, 13 ships sunk, four probables and three damaged in this series of actions.

Other blows to the Japanese as a result of the increased air war in the Pacific were many. On September 3, 12 ships were sunk or damaged off Mindanao in the Philippines.

In a raid on the Celebes 15 Japanese planes were destroyed.

On September 6 an Allied task force attacked Palau, west of the Carolines, and left 17 small ships burning.

---

strength for the last advance.

Three Allied armies, moving on a 225-mile front, are preparing for a triple thrust from France and Belgium.

British armour and infantry have crossed the Albert Canal in Belgium—25 miles from Germany. Sedan, dominating the gap through which the Germans invaded France in 1940, has been taken.

The Siegfried Line

The Moselle river has been crossed and the battle for the Lorraine gap is flaring up. German resistance stiffens nearer the Siegfried Line.

Further south the Allies are only 50 miles short of Belfort—another door to the Reich.

The Red Army is again on the offensive towards the former Polish Corridor. The Riga-Warsaw line has been dented. Fighting between Russia and Finland has ended.

Sweden leads the neutrals in refusing refuge to war criminals.

---

jungles of Burma east of the Chindwin, after their disastrous flight across the river.

The Japanese, using the river route to escape, are heading south in anything available from paddle-steamers to makeshift rafts.

Fourteenth Army troops, clearing the west bank of the Chindwin, have found thousands of Jap skeletons. They are what is left of the "Invade India" army, which took this year the biggest defeat the Japanese have had.

No official increase has yet been made to the month old figure released of 50,000 Japanese killed in the fighting on all Burma fronts.

Allied soldiers have now cleared the Tiddim road, for 110 miles south of Imphal.

The air-war on the retreating Japanese continues. They are being bombed and strafed in their temporary camps, on the roads and on the rivers.

Curtains for Hitler

IT'S curtains for Hitler any time now. The five-year melodrama is drawing to its bloody end—and it will be an end that will make the final scene of Hamlet look like the vicar's tea-party.

That's the message we bring you through South East Asia Command in another VICTORY NEWS. It's carried to you by planes that are making the Japs feel much as the Germans are feeling.

And the way the Japs feel now is nothing to the way they're going to feel when all the men and material that have smashed Germany are brought out here.

They're Waiting For You

THIS IS HOW THEY LIVE AND WORK IN ENGLAND NOW

HOW are they at home? That's the biggest question you're asking and may be those 25-word postcards don't give much an answer. So here is a bit more news:

The answer is "All's well" —and you need not wonder any more. The lights are beginning to shine again, firewatchers are disbanding and even the Home Guard parade only because they like it, and not because they have to.

Compulsion is "off". The tension is over back home. But it has begun out here. But for the Japs and not for us.

* Women and Children first

Don't worry about your families. All they lack is

Price control is working well. The Black Market is smacked down.

Civvy Britain makes both ends meet.

* Home Towns Don't Alter

Even after five years of bombs there isn't much change in the everyday look of things. Houses and shops are shabbier. There has been no paint to spare these last few years. Camouflage came first.

But the old life goes on. Theatres are doing big business. London and the bigger provincial towns have "better than ever" shows—though choruses are not so young as they were. Cinemas are doing as well as ever.

There is still plenty of

babies get extra. There is plenty of food—more than there used to be. Little 'luxuries like oranges and lemons are obtainable in the shops again.

Clothes rationing goes on. There are no silk stockings for your wives and girl friends. They get no make-up either. But they still manage to look pretty good. Why? Because morale "is up on top".

* War Jobs and Price Control

Arms, ammunition, kit—war work drives ahead. There is no slackening just because "it's in the bag", in Europe. The folk at home are keeping the wheels turning full pressure to give US the weapons to set YOU free. And that won't be long now.

It has never been so true to say that woman's work is never done. Women make guns, shells and bombs, grease railway engines, grow crops, and deliver the letters.

not quite the sort of beer we used to know. Gin, rum and some wine is to be had, but there is very little whisky. Maybe they are saving it for us—and for you.

* There's Still Some Sport

Sport keeps going. But as big crowds can seldom travel to watch it is on a reduced scale. Even so they ran the Derby again this year (at Newmarket as is usual in wartime). The winner was Ocean Swell, a 20-1 outsider owned by Lord Rosebery. W. Nevett, the Yorkshire jockey, took the ride, instead of the stable jockey, E. Smith.

Wembley had a Cup Final again and Chelsea beat Charlton before a crowd of 60,000, including the King and Princess Elizabeth. Cricket 'Tests' have been going on all the summer between British sides and Services teams from the Dominions. You'll be seeing them yourselves soon.

The boys are on the job. The Japs are already scared stiff. So keep smiling. We're on our way!

BARBED WIRE IS DOWN

All Britain's beaches are now open to seaside holiday-makers.

There are no longer any special defence areas—except to aliens.

The miles of barbed wire which made the seashore round most of Britain "out of bounds" is now coming down.

When travel eases we can expect seaside holidays to be popular again—the no-swimming ban and the fact that children couldn't build sand castles made them rather pointless.

The military authorities still reserve the right in some areas to stop the public should the need arise. The people of Britain consider that fair enough.

special address by the Group Commander, Colonel Nagatomo, in which he congratulated them on their work in building the railway. A second prepared speech then followed, this time addressed to the souls of the men of the Group (there were nearly a 1,000 by this time) who had died while working for their Imperial Japanese masters. The text of Nagatomo's oration ended with the words, 'Please accept my deepest sympathy and regards and may you sleep peacefully and eternally.' The Japanese order for the memorial services to be held, their participation in them and in particular such speeches as that of Nagatomo were generally regarded as supreme examples of Japanese hypocrisy. This was a natural reaction on the part of the men who had seen so many of their comrades die, but it did not really uncover the meaning of the Japanese actions, which were more an expression of respect for the death of the prisoners in fulfilling the Imperial will; their callous military ethic saw no particular value in individual human life.

The completion of the railway brought an inevitable slackening in the pace of work in the camps along its course; but the six-month 'speedo' had already claimed thousands of lives, and its after-effects were to demand many more in the following months, though it seemed at last that the bulk of the prisoners might yet win the fight to survive which had been their principal concern ever since the first transfers to Burma and Siam had started. It was now too late, however, for the majority of the Asian labourers who had formed the larger, but less effective part of the railway force. The Tamils, Javanese, Chinese and Burmese had been struck down in their thousands by dysentery, malaria and cholera, and also by sheer fatalistic resignation to death. The chaotic conditions prevailing in their camps and the inadequacy of their medical provisions have already been recounted, but it was principally be-

cause they were leaderless and unorganised that the Asian workers had suffered so severely. They had been torn from their social setting in the plantations of Malaya or the paddy fields of Burma by the pressures of economic necessity and the cynical confidence tricks of the Japanese, and thrust into a totally alien environment where they had to fend entirely for themselves. There, without guidance, leadership or discipline beyond brutal beatings from the Japanese, their social cohesion had quickly disintegrated. Over a quarter of a million Asians had moved to Siam and Burma to help their Japanese brethren to build the 'Co-prosperity Sphere', but when the railway was completed only a pitiful remnant was left. The rest had become the innocent victims of the larger struggle between the imperial powers. It should be remembered, however, that just as they were a sacrifice to the Japanese single-minded pursuit of a purely strategic policy, they were equally the unsought oblation of the western powers to the gods of commercial success and financial normalcy. Throughout the 1920s and early '30s proper security arrangements for the eastern Empires had received little consideration and no priority from the metropolitan governments, who retired behind the convenient but unrealistic ideals of the League of Nations and World Disarmament. If the peoples of South East Asia were to suffer most from the policies of both protagonists, it is hardly surprising that when the war was over they should have expressed a wish to run their own affairs.

In November 1943, with the railway now operating, the Japanese began a major redeployment and reorganisation of the POWs who had done most of the building of it, re-locating the major camps at the new line's southern end. Among the first of the European prisoners to begin the move south were the survivors of 'F' and 'H' Forces whose time on the railway had been briefer than that of any other prisoner group, but who had suffered more grievously than the rest. It seems that these two forces had never formed a permanent part of the railway organisation, but had merely been on loan from Malaya Command to the Siam garrison forces for the period of feverish activity that followed the decision to complete the project sooner than originally intended. They had therefore suffered the worst treatment in the worst areas of the trace, and now, broken and decimated by their ordeal, they were to be unceremoniously returned to Changi and their legitimate masters. The one consolation for the men of these groups was that they did not have to march back to their transit base at Kanchanaburi but went via the railroad they had built. Kanchanaburi had by this time been built up as a sort of makeshift hospital at which the two groups were collected together and given some semblance of medical treatment before being returned to Singapore. Living conditions were certainly better there and once again the food situation was eased by the presence of Thai traders, but the camp became progressively more crowded as further survivors from the up-country camps swelled its numbers.

The fit men in the camp, who were issued with fresh clothing and footwear and at last got some rest, were well off by comparison with the sick, for the hospital accommodation was hopelessly inadequate. An Australian prisoner calculated that into an area 150 paces wide by 370 paces long, 2,300 sick men were crowded. Some of the patients were quite beyond hope, so wasted by disease and malnutrition that they added little to the weight of the stretchers on which they were borne, and as before, though expert medical attention was available for all the sick, the shortage of drugs precluded rapid cures. Indeed the journies down from the jungle camps, particularly those of 'F' Force which

were furthest away, were hurried and badly organised and caused further deaths among patients who were quite unfit to travel. 'F' and 'H' Forces had numbered a little over 10,000 men when they had left Singapore in April and May, but by December their numbers were reduced by almost 4,000. 'F' Force had lost 3,096 men, forty-four per cent of its original strength, while 'H' Force deaths totalled 885, twenty-seven per cent of its initial complement. One 'H' Force survivor who convalesced at Tamarkan and Kanchanaburi considered himself one of the fortunate ones. He now weighed eight stone ten lbs against his normal fourteen stone, and during his eight months in Siam he had suffered from beri-beri, pellagra, dengue fever, malaria, dysentery, blackwater fever, jaundice, scabies, ringworm, tropical ulcers, tropical pamphlicus and tinia rash. His case was not untypical.

After a relatively short stay in the base camps around Kanchanaburi, 'F' and 'H' Forces continued their journey to Singapore, resuming their acquaintance with the inevitable steel box cars which had taken them up to Ban Pong. This time conditions were slightly better, the men were allocated only twenty to a truck and some of these even presented the luxury of straw bale furnishings; but it was a mournful journey nonetheless, punctuated by tragic halts for the burial of many of those who had been denied a longer period for recuperation at Kanchanaburi. Always the trains were stopped and the Japanese guards waited patiently, apparently anxious that the bodies should receive in death the respect that had been denied to them in life. At one period a train a day was leaving Kanchanaburi for Singapore, the most desperately ill being taken direct to Changi, the rest to other camps in the area, all to be greeted by the shocked astonishment of the 6,000-odd who had spent all their captivity on the island, troubled by their own undernourished conditions, and yet fit men as compared with their erstwhile comrades who now rejoined them and of whose tribulations they had hitherto been in blissful ignorance. One observer who witnessed their return recorded the sight as follows: 'They were in a shocking condition, suffering from serious attacks of beri-beri, malaria, tropical ulcers and extreme debility. The loss of weight was simply appalling, averaging about seventy lbs per individual; eighty per cent of them had to be admitted at once to hospital.' There in Changi, the survivors of 'F' and 'H' Forces remained until the Japanese surrender.

Shortly afterwards, in the last days of December 1943, the two groups of Burma-based railway prisoners began their journey to base camps in Siam. All the European railway workers were now being concentrated in a series of large camps at the railway's southern end between Chungkai, the first major camp on the Khwae Noi river, and Nakhon Pathom a few miles east of Ban Pong. Tamarkan was the headquarters camp for No 3 Group from Burma into which the smaller No 5 Group was incorporated, though some ex-Burma men were also found at Kanchanaburi or the new hospital camp at Nakhon Pathom. For the men from the camps in Burma their transfer to Tamarkan produced an immediate improvement in the food situation. In a single day the prisoners here received more green vegetables in their ration than they had seen in months in the jungle, and the evening meals actually contained pieces of meat, fish and egg. The canteen also provided bananas, eggs and occasionally, for those who could afford them, roast ducks. To men who had come from the desolation and miseries of the jungle Tamarkan seemed indeed a land of milk and honey; the wretched atap huts with their bamboo sleeping platforms were still the same, and men still died from the after effects of their jungle experiences, but at least the prisoners

at Tamarkan were not starving. However only 9,808 of their original force of 11,537 were able to share the improvements at Tamarkan; the rest lay in graves along the railway trace between Thanbyuzayat and the Three Pagodas Pass.

Chungkai was the destination for the parties of No 2 Group, which had started its railway work at just over

Above and over page: **POWs perform an operation in the newly-opened operating theatre at Chungkai hospital**

8,900 strong but was now reduced by 7,540, of whom 2,000 lay sick in its base hospital. The hospital was large and efficiently run and had separate wards for the dysentery and malaria cases, and another for those patients whose ulcerated legs had required amputation. It even boasted a remedial PT Centre where crippled and deformed limbs were coaxed back into

operation. The whole camp at Chungkai was divided into two parts, the Red half for the fit men and the Blue for the sick. Of course the hospital contained many of the Blue patients, but there was also a separate Blue

119

camp for those who would have been in hospital under normal circumstances, but who at Chungkai merely took as much rest as they could and attempted to recover by their own efforts. They were helped a little by Chungkai's flourishing canteen which sold a variety of food dishes. The whole camp was surrounded by a slender bamboo fence just inside of which ran an exercise path whose circular perimeter measured about one and a quarter miles.

On reorganisation the men of No 4 Group steadily filtered back to their base camp at Tamuang, a few miles south of Kanchanaburi. This group was the largest to work on the railway and when at full strength it had numbered 13,700 men, but by the time the last parties had arrived back from the jungle and the group was finally concentrated, it had suffered over 2,000 deaths. Soon after the railway had been completed advance parties had been sent down to Tamuang to enlarge it so that it could accommodate 10,000 men. The expansion was a hurried and makeshift affair, but the camp was clean and well laid-out and the work for once was particularly light. Life at Tamuang soon settled into a fairly peaceful routine disturbed only by the Japanese guards' insistence on holding frequent *tenkos* or roll calls which, as at most camps, were generally so badly organised that they became an interminable tedium for the prisoners. Nevertheless, Tamuang had its compensations; it was situated in what had once been a tobacco plantation and from the few stray plants that still grew around the compound, a cigar-making industry soon developed among the men, while the additional food supplies brought from the local villagers, together with ducks stolen from the Japanese-run duck farm, brought a little more protein to the diet and a consequent general improvement in health.

However, it was not long before the Japanese found other labouring jobs

for large numbers of tne POWs who were enjoying their well-earned respite in the base camps. Some indeed had never left the railway, being kept there for maintenance work, and it was not long before parties were sent up from the base camps to join them. These groups ranged in strength from 150 to 600 and were sent up the line to do repair work, for breakdowns

resulting from natural hazards, jerry-building and deliberate sabotage were not infrequent. Other chores were cutting wood fuel for the locomotives and handling stores at dumps along the line. At first, conditions in the maintenance camps were not unduly severe, but as the number of men decreased, because of the toll taken by disease, they rapidly worsened. Be-

sides, the numbers employed on the railway was now too small to encourage merchants to visit the line with supplies, and in some camps there was a occurrence of the brutalities that had recurred in 1943, with sick men being beaten and driven out to work. In fact the only redeeming feature of the camps was the relative facility with which the

seriously ill could be evacuated to the base areas in the returning trains. Two other wretched groups of prisoners were sent off on road-building projects in areas where the conditions were particularly bad. One party of 1,000 men was employed making a road through virgin jungle across the Tenasserim peninsula between Pra-chuab and Mergui. Their accommodation was appalling and the food poor and within five months twenty-five per cent of the party had died. The other group was a British-Dutch battalion of 400 which was sent from Tamuang to build a road leading westwards from the railway at Wampo to Tavoy on the coast. The survivors

Ulcer operation

and gruelling labour that only extended nursing in the intensive care unit
of a modern hospital would have kept
them from an early grave. Such
facilities were inevitably not available
in Japanese-occupied Siam, but the
authorities did make some attempt to
organise a general base hospital at a
place called Nakhon Pathom which
lay a short distance away from the
railway on the route to Bangkok.
The Nakhon Pathom hospital became
one of the largest ever established,
having at one time some 8,000 patients,
with an average strength of 5,000 including all the chronically sick and
maimed from the various groups
employed on the railway. By the end
of January 1944 hospital staffs and
workers had been despatched from
all the other camps to open up this
new POW hospital. The chief medical
officer was an Australian doctor, a
consultant surgeon in civil life, and
with him operated a team of thirty-
four doctors, Australian, American,
British and Dutch who met twice a
week to discuss their many problems
and to pool their individual specialist
knowledge and ingenuity. Their
achievements were remarkable. At
Nakhon Pathom 1,500 blood transfusions with defibrinated blood were
given to ease the scourge of an-
aemia induced by chronic malnutrition, while the surgeons carried
out nearly 1,000 major operations of
all kinds. Excellent artificial limbs
were made and fitted to the many
men whose legs had been amputated
because of the spread of tropical
ulcers. By the time Japan capitu-
lated the total number of stretcher
cases had been reduced to 400, and of
the 10,000 patients brought to this
hospital, the total mortality was only
2.8 per cent, remarkably low in view
of its primitive conditions and lack
of proper medical supplies. A main
factor in its success was the eking out
of a supply of drugs and medical
materials received from the American
Red Cross in May 1944.

of this force were eventually picked
up by the Allies in 1945 in a worse
physical condition than almost any
others recovered from Siam.

Even among the thousands of men
whose railway ordeal was now over,
there were many who were so weakened by disease and undernourish-
ment, or broken by harsh treatment

Impermanent way

The major reorganisation of the prisoners had been completed by early 1944 when, with the departure of the survivors of 'F' and 'H' Forces to Singapore, a total of about 43,000 men was concentrated in the six main camps around Kanchanaburi: one on each arm of the rivers at Chungkai and Tamarkan, one at Tamuang, two a little distance away from the railway at Non Pladuk and Nakhon Pathom on the main line to Bangkok, and one at the town of Kanchanaburi itself. With the improvement in the general standard of food and the absence of major work projects, the POWs might have been excused for fondly believing that the worst of their sufferings were over and that they simply had to wait out the remainder of the war until they were liberated by the advancing Allied armies. It rapidly became clear, however, that the Japanese had other plans for many of them, and as for the prospect of their release by the Allies, the realisation steadily grew among many prisoners that the Japanese, rather than surrender their charges to the Allies before they themselves withdrew or were killed, might extend to their charges the Nipponese belief that death was preferable to dishonour, and massacre them wholesale.

The Japanese soon made it clear that they intended to ship 10,000 of the fittest prisoners to undertake further service to their Imperial masters in mainland Japan, supplementing the labour force of women and young people who were now being used for industrial work while the men defended the far-flung and crumbling Empire. The men for the Japan parties were first selected and inspected by their own medical officers and then subjected to a second scrutiny by the Japanese. Finally, they were divided up into groups of 150 with one officer to each group, and issued with warm clothes for the colder Japanese climate. These were mainly Allied heavy uniforms which the Japanese had collected from a variety of sources and the men who now wore them looked more like the cast of a musical comedy than prisoners preparing for the second great ordeal of their captivity: some were in battle dress, others in naval hospital trousers, tartan trews, air force jackets or the grey flannel shirts normally worn by Indian troops.

The efforts of the Japanese to get this labour force to the homeland give some idea of the desperate straits to which their merchant shipping had now been reduced by Allied bombing and submarine action, although the war still had a further sixteen months to run. Between April and June 1944, 10,000 prisoners were collected at Saigon for shipment to Japan, but because of the scarcity of shipping many of them were transferred by rail to Singapore in the hope that a boat might be available for them there. Already in Singapore were other groups of ex-railway prisoners who had been sent there direct from the Siam base camps. The River Valley camp was used as the transit area for the Japan-bound prisoners, but as with the Saigon parties, many of those collected in Singapore did not leave the island until after the Japanese capitulation. Those who were unfortunate enough finally to embark had the

A direct hit on the approach to a railway viaduct

daunting experience of running the gauntlet of attacks by their own submarines, and hundreds were drowned when their ships went down.

One of the early parties to leave Singapore sailed in a small convoy of six ships, three merchantmen and three warships. Two of the merchantmen, which fortunately were not carrying prisoners, were torpedoed and sunk, while the third, an old Dutch cargo-boat built in Rotterdam in 1909 and crammed with 2,500 European prisoners and 750 Javanese coolies, emerged from the attack unscathed. From this time onwards few convoys for Japan got through without losses and the authorities were forced to press into service ancient craft which were not really fit for an ocean voyage. On 1st July, for example, a party of prisoners left Singapore aboard an ancient British freighter, built at the turn of the century, and which had already suffered from a bombing attack in Java. Much of the superstructure of the centre section of the ship, including the bridge, had been burnt out, and two long steel building girders ran from stem to stern, one on each side of the ship, serving the vital purpose of holding its two halves together. The improvised wheelhouse,

Above: **Japanese merchant ship sunk by USS** *Drum.* *Above right:* **A Japanese patrol boat goes to the bottom.** *Right:* **British and Australian survivors are rescued by USS** *Sealion*

a low bamboo structure, gave no view of the sea ahead of the craft, the steersman having to rely for guidance on verbal instructions passed by intermediaries from a sailor stationed in the prow. The use of such dilapidated craft inevitably meant poor travelling conditions for the POWs, and these miseries were aggravated by recurrences of malaria for which no treatment was available since few ships carried sufficient quinine, while in some cases the food was so bad that even members of the Japanese crews went down with beri-beri.

Of all the ordeals, the risk of submarine attack by their own countrymen was the hardest to bear, adding the dimension of psychological strain to bodies already sorely ravaged. One convoy of thirty-eight ships, which contained at least one shipload of prisoners from the railway, left Singapore on 4th July and was attacked by submarines almost continuously from leaving Formosa till it was within twelve hours sailing

time of Kyushu, the southernmost of the Japanese islands. Of course, the later the departure date from Singapore or Saigon, the worse was the submarine threat and the danger of attack by bombers, for both elements in the Allied armoury were becoming stronger with each passing week. A force of 2,300 prisoners, under the command of Brigadier Varley, sailed from Singapore on 6th September aboard two transports, the *Kachidoki Maru* and the *Rokyo Maru*, in a convoy which finally totalled fifteen vessels. Early on the 12th the convoy was attacked by American submarines; an escort vessel was sunk first, then two tankers and finally the *Rokyu Maru*. The other prisoner-ship went down the following night. Some of the survivors were picked up by Japanese vessels, but 141 men from the *Rokyu Maru* were in the water, clinging to life rafts and wreckage, some for as long as five days, before they were finally rescued by US submarines which hurried to the scene from as far away as 200 miles when they learned of the disaster. From these survivors the Allied nations received the first authentic accounts of the conditions of the prisoners held in Burma and Siam. But nearly 1,500 of the men who had survived those conditions were drowned in the attacks on this convoy. However, many of the ex-railway prisoners did reach Japan, but life there was not much of an improvement since the work in the coal and copper mines and shipyards was hard, the winters were desperately cold and the food grew steadily worse. As the blockade tightened even the supply of rice ran out in some areas and only coarse millet from Korea and edible seaweed were available to replace it.

The tragic experiences of some of the parties sent to Japan provide fragmentary evidence of the progressive attrition upon one end of the communication system in which the Burma-Siam railway was intended to be so vital a link. By the end of the second full year of the Pacific War the US submarine campaign was in full swing, and the mercantile marine had lost a further 434 ships, a total of one and three quarter million tons, and in the first three months of 1944 the sinkings rose to a crescendo, trebling the average monthly losses of the previous year. The sea passage to Bangkok grew steadily more precarious and the ships available rapidly dwindled in number, for the Japanese had no reserve ship-building capacity to call upon and they were very slow to introduce a convoy system, for which in any case they were unable to provide sufficient escort craft. Besides it was not a static threat that they were dealing with, but one that became more menacing as the months passed, easily outpacing the defensive measures which they belatedly introduced. Eventually, ships were no longer safe even in Bangkok coastal waters, for by the end of 1943 American Liberator bombers were extending their raids as far as the major port of Siam and had already attacked the dock area, wrecking its installations with 500-lb bombs. At the start of 1944 the Allies also began mining Bangkok harbour, sinking several ships and delaying others as the hard-pressed Japanese minesweepers struggled to get to grips with the problem. The transfer of shipping to other minor ports in the area proved no solution, for the Liberators were soon mining these as well, undertaking round trips equivalent in distance to a flight from London to Naples in order to disrupt the supply route to Burma.

In Burma itself the railway system was also being attacked in raids that were all the heavier for the lack of other suitable tactical targets, and the more successful because of the railway's two inherent weaknesses: a lack of side lines over which traffic might be run if the yards of such

RAF Liberators attack the Burma section of the railway

centres as Pegu and Mandalay were incapacitated, and the large number of bridges which were very vulnerable to attack. Burma had a total of 126 railway bridges that were over 100 feet long and a further 176 of more than forty feet in length, and the successful bombing of any two such bridges therefore isolated the intervening track and opened to destruction the trapped rolling stock. Operations against the whole system were co-ordinated between the British squadrons and Tenth US Army Air Force, heavy bombers of the former attacking by night and the latter by day. The attacks upon engines and rolling stock resulted in the destruction or damage of over 150 locomotives during the latter half of 1943, hundreds of trucks were destroyed, and at the same time there were always several bridges out of action. Meanwhile marshalling yards, repair depôts and turntables were also being constantly attacked, reducing the flexibility of what remained of the railway system

and slowing down the process of repair and maintenance. The net result of this bombing within Burma, and of the sinkings on the high seas was that the new railway, which was designed to link the two, was deprived of much of its usefulness even before it started operating, and no sooner was it open to traffic than it began to suffer heavy attacks itself to add to the break-downs, derailments and bridge faults that already menaced its 260 miles of makeshift track, many stretches of which could scarcely be dignified with the name of 'permanent way'.

The Allies were soon aware that the Burma-Siam railway had been constructed, and while this knowledge did not lessen the intensity of their attacks on the domestic rail routes of Burma, it did bring into strategic prominence their relationship to the new line. Accordingly, raids on the junction point at Thanbyuzayat were started and the railway from there into Burma proper, via the ferry terminals at Moulmein and Martaban

well as on the pens and shelters which the Japanese had now built to protect their engines. Spiked bombs were also a valuable addition to the Allied armoury since they were particularly good at tearing up stretches of the track.

This onslaught made repair and maintenance work a dangerous and an arduous business for the parties who were sent up the line periodically from the camps. On one occasion a train crammed full of prisoners was caught in the open and bombed with great accuracy by Allied aircraft, causing over 100 casualties of whom forty-one were killed. However, the situation was even worse for those prisoners who were crowded into base camps located dangerously near to what were obviously particularly important bombing targets, especially the vital bridges over the Mae Khlong at Tamarkan, and the Non Pladuk area further south which was a main maintenance centre for the railway and, in addition, lay close to the junction with the main Singapore-Bangkok line. The main camp at Non Pladuk lay amid the marshalling yards, workshops and supply sheds of the railway depôt and close to an ack-ack battery. It therefore seemed inevitable that if the Allied planes struck heavily at the depôt the prisoners would again be in danger; nevertheless, the Japanese had forbidden the digging of slit trenches and when on 6th September 1944 the first wave of twenty-one Liberators appeared over the area the prisoners were all crowded into their huts, perhaps confident that the accuracy of bombing techniques would enable the camp to be spared. Indeed the first wave did bomb with great precision, but the last plane of the second flight appeared to release its bombs too soon and the stick fell right across the flimsy bamboo camp killing ninety-eight prisoners and injuring 330 more. The Japanese commander refused to

and the Sittang bridge at Mokpalin, was heavily pounded. As time went on more and more of the new strategic railway came under attack, the energy with which the Japanese attempted to defend it and keep it open giving fresh evidence of the damage and delay which the raids were causing. What the Allied pilots did not appreciate, however, was that the repair of damaged bridges and track was being carried out by prisoners of war, and that the further south they struck with their bombing raids, the more the lives of the prisoners were once again being put at risk. The raids decreased during the 1944 monsoon when flying conditions were hazardous and when aircraft were in any case diverted to other uses, but they burst out again with a fresh violence in October and November when strengthened squadrons took on the new railway as their prime target. Besides bombers, Beaufighters were now getting to the line and were proving especially useful for attacks on locomotives and rolling stock as

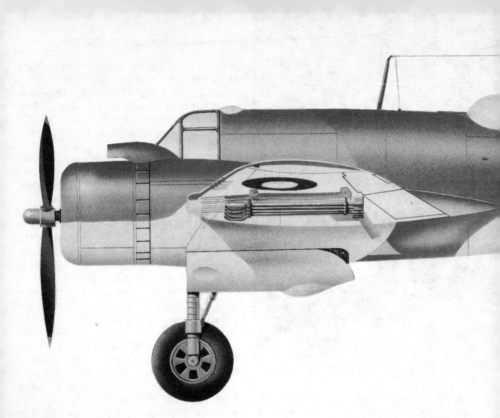

Below: The Consolidated PB4Y-1
This US Navy patrol bomber was a modified B-24J Liberator, adapted to long patrols over water. The type was also used in some numbers over South-East Asia as it had a long range and was particularly reliable. *Engines:* Four Pratt & Whitney R-1830 radials, 1,200hp each. *Armament:* Ten ·5-inch Browning machine guns and up to 12,800lbs of bombs (only on very short missions) or 5,000lbs over maximum range. *Speed:* 300mph at 30,000 feet. *Climb:* 25 minutes to 20,000 feet. *Ceiling:* 36,000 feet. *Range:* 2,100 miles with 5,000lbs of bombs. *Weight empty/ loaded:* 36,500/65,000lbs. *Span:* 110 feet. *Length:* 67 feet 2 inches. *Crew:* 12

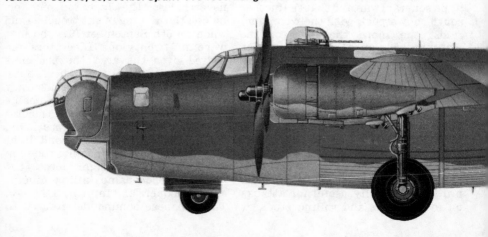

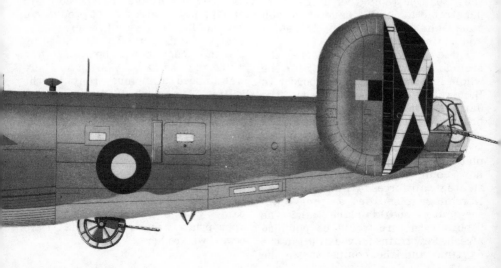

The Bristol Beaufighter VIF was the version of the Beaufighter most widely used by the RAF in India and Burma, the first squadron to use the type becoming operational in January 1943. The type was admirably suited for operations in South-East Asia as it was relatively fast in comparison with Japanese fighters, extremely rugged and very powerfully armed, especially when it used rocket armament. *Engines:* Two Bristol Hercules VI or XVI radials, 1,670hp each. *Armament:* Four 20mm Hispano cannon with 240 rounds per gun and six .303-inch Browning machine guns with 1,000 rounds per gun (or four 20mm cannon and eight 90-lb rockets) plus two 250-lb bombs. *Speed:* 333mph at 15,600 feet. *Ceiling:* 26,500 feet. *Range:* 1,480 miles normal, 1,810 miles maximum. *Weight empty/loaded:* 14,600/21,600lbs. *Span:* 57 feet 10 inches. *Length:* 41 feet 8 inches. *Crew:* Two. *Role:* Long range strike fighter

sanction the move of the camp to a safer area, 'This will happen many times again,' he said, 'You are soldiers, you must be prepared to die.' However, he did finally permit slit trenches to be dug, but the camp itself stayed put and the whole area was frequently strafed and bombed. A similar heavy raid on the Tamarkan bridges took place at the end of November, and once again the POWs were inevitably among the casualties since their camp lay close to the ack-ack battery defending the railway bridge. Most of the bombs effectively plastered the battery, but three overcarried and demolished the ends of two of the prisoners' huts killing seventeen and wounding a further sixty. When the POW authorities complained about the camp being located so close to the ack-ack battery the Japanese replied with their impenetrable logic, 'We have given you guns right beside the camp to defend you against the planes'.

These heavy attacks were the prelude to a mass onslaught on the whole line from the Burma border to Bangkok, which lasted until the Japanese capitulation. The major bridges were repeatedly broken up and much of the rolling stock was destroyed; as soon as repairs were completed on one particular bridge the fact would be reported back to the strategic air forces by what one of the Korean guards called a 'come-look-see-go-back-speakie-plane', and the rebuilt structure would be pounded afresh. Few trains moved at all in the daytime and the confusion on the

Above: **The rocket-armed Bristol Beaufighter, ideal for attacks on rolling stock.** *Right:* **A 200-foot prisoner-built bridge is shattered by a low level Liberator attack**

single line track was appalling. It sometimes took a month for goods to travel the 350 miles from Bangkok to Moulmein. But while Allied reports could call these results 'spectacular,' other adjectives might have been chosen by the prisoners who were helpless in the face of the attacks, their camps unmarked, unannounced and all overcrowded. Many men found the attacks more terrifying than anything they had experienced during their captivity; the feeling of being trapped and being ignorantly pounded by their own people after three years of Japanese maltreatment produced a sense of helplessness and despondency that was only partially alleviated by the knowledge that the bombings were rendering the railway useless. There was indeed a vicious irony in the killing of men who had successfully survived the jungle nightmare, by the very agents to whom they looked for liberation. Late in 1944 the planes started dropping pamphlets over the camp areas with news of the war and messages of encouragement for the prisoners. One pamphlet ended, 'Take heart, we are coming!,' but as one camp wag put it, it might more appropriately have concluded 'Take cover, we are here.'

Deliverance

As 1945 approached there were other factors besides the bombing which were causing disquiet among the prisoners; food was becoming more scarce and the Japanese authorities were growing increasingly intractable. Given the Japanese temperament, it was scarcely likely that the news of disastrous reverses for their forces in every part of the Empire would result in any improvement in the lot of their prisoners of war. But it was not merely this increased testiness that began to concern the men; what worried them more was the possibility that they might never be liberated at all but be massacred by the Japanese if the possibility of whole-sale defeat or withdrawal faced their armies in South East Asia.

It became clear towards the end of 1944 that the prison authorities had received orders to secure all the camps, enclosing the prisoners who had hitherto been restricted in their movements only by the threat of punishment or death if caught escaping by the acute shortage of food and by the great distances that separated them from the nearest Allied sanctuaries. The men now had to dig deep moats around their camps with high embankments beyond them blocking their view of the surrounding countryside, and, as an additional precaution, a series of fences were constructed of both barbed wire and bamboo. Sentry posts were also built and so placed as to cover the entire camp boundaries. Of course, this could have been merely an additional precaution against escape, or an effort to prevent illicit trading with local villagers, but there was also the possibility that it was

Clearing the Japanese from Assam: a tank crosses a river north of Imphal

Men of the 26th Indian Division search surrendered Japanese

Field-Marshal (here General) Count Terauchi, C-in-C Southern Army

of Japan was now inevitable and yet there was no sign that her armies would do other than fight to the death despite the hopelessness of their position. By early 1945 the situation of the Japanese Burma Area Army was desperate; in the middle of the previous year its Fifteenth Army had been virtually destroyed in the battle of Imphal, where it lost over 53,000 men, while in March 1945 the bulk of the Area Army was irreparably shattered on the Mandalay Plain, the loss of Rangoon following two months later. Nevertheless, these heavy defeats yielded comparatively few prisoners, fewer still unwounded ones, and the Japanese were clearly planning to fight on in South East Asia despite these major reverses; such at least was the impression gained by the prisoners as they watched the intensive bayonet and rifle practice of their guards.

In June 1945 a party of 500 prisoners was sent back up the line to build a defensive position a few miles south of the Three Pagodas Pass. The work was extremely gruelling and the men were driven with the same kind of feverish haste as had characterised the earlier 'speedo' working, and towards the end the men were putting in eighteen-hour shifts. The same month it was announced that the officers' camp was to be moved again, this time well away from the railway, to Nakhon Nayok, a small township at the foot of the mountains about seventy miles north-east of Bangkok. There, it appeared, the officers were to build a new camp right in the middle of a Japanese defence line which was reported to be held by about 30,000 troops. This sounded very much like the site of Japan's last stand for the defence of Siam, and with Allied bombers becoming daily more numerous it did not promise to be a healthy spot for a POW camp.

The advance party of prisoners moved off to Nakhon Nayok at the end of June, and the following month the main body began to follow in

designed to facilitate the liquidation of the prisoners who would have been at best an unnecessary encumbrance and at worst an additional threat, in the event of an Allied landing in Siam. Furthermore, in January the Japanese began to separate officer prisoners from their men, moving them all into the enlarged camp at Kanchanaburi, except for a proportion of the medical officers who stayed behind with the soldiers. This action was perhaps a belated decision to conform to one of the provisions of the Geneva Convention previously ignored by the authorities; equally it could have been interpreted as an attempt to minimise co-ordinated resistance by the prisoners should they try to overpower their guards at some stage, or defend themselves against a possible massacre. It is not surprising that many prisoners later confessed to feeling more on edge during their last few months of captivity than at any other time. The ultimate defeat

Admiral Lord Louis Mountbatten talks to General 'Vinegar Joe' Stilwell

parties of 400 at five-day intervals. It proved to be wretched journey and a very poor camp hacked out of virgin jungle by the first parties to arrive. It lay two miles from the main road to which a connecting track had to be built, and from which the camp supplies had to be carried each day. Many officers did this trip barefoot five times a day and carrying loads of anything up to one hundred lbs. Some of the other camps were on the move as well, parties leaving the railway to construct defence works for the Japanese in positions to the south and east. In May, the group at Tamuang left for Pratchai, 110 miles away on the other side of Bangkok where they camped alongside a battalion of troops training very intensively, and worked at preparing defensive positions. It was here, too, that a Korean guard intimated to one of the camp medical officers that the Japanese planned to kill all their prisoners. As at Nakhon Nayok and Kanchanaburi, where there were still a number of officers, news came in more and more frequently of losses and reverses suffered by the

Japanese, and the restlessness and tension in the camps mounted. The local situation also appeared to be turning against the Japanese forces, for parties of local natives and guerillas had begun attacking isolated posts and individual soldiers; moreover, the Korean guards, always abominably treated by their superiors were growing restive. It was a situation in which one might have expected the Japanese to strike out like a wounded animal, meting out the vengeance of history not on the European powers whom they plainly had no chance of defeating, but on the thousands of 'dishonoured' white prisoners whose lives they still controlled and who were now a possible danger as well as a nuisance.

This was indeed precisely the action which the Japanese were preparing to take; in the headquarters of Field Marshal Count Terauchi's Southern Army at Saigon plans already existed for the massacre of all prisoners and

internees if the invasion of South
East Asia should begin in earnest.
Admiral Mountbatten intended to
start his invasion early in September,
and his assault was to be preceded by
the bombing of Japanese strongpoints
and troop concentrations, near to
which many of the prisoners were
grouped. It seemed that events were
moving inexorably to a climax for
these wretched men, having survived
the 'railway of death' they were
either to be bombed by their friends or
butchered by their captors. Consequently, there was great surprise
and enormous relief in the Siamese
prison camps when the senior Allied
officers in each camp were informed
by the Japanese authorities on 16th
August 1945 that the war was over

and they were now free men. 'His
Imperial Highness, the Emperor of
Japan, has decided to stop fighting,'
announced the Japanese commander
of all the prisoner groups, 'You will
soon go home. We are responsible for
your safety until you go. You can
sing your national anthem and hoist
your flags.' And there was not a
liberating Allied soldier in sight.

This remarkable *volte-face* by the
Japanese command in South East
Asia, reflecting as it did decisions
taken by the Imperial Cabinet, was
only partly the result of the worsening
military situation in the southern
regions and the increasing devastation and hardship at home. It is
true that by this time the islands of
Japan were totally isolated from those

taken alive out of a garrison of 21,000 troops, and the first seventy days of the bitter struggle for Okinawa yielded an average of less than four prisoners captured each day; in all 72,500 men out of a garrison of 80,000 preferred death to surrender, despite a US propaganda campaign involving the dropping of 8,000,000 leaflets designed to persuade the garrison to give up.

It was with a similar blind determination that Terauchi of Southern Army continued to reconstruct and strengthen the defences of Siam in the first days of August 1945. Then came the triple hammer blows of the atomic bombing of Hiroshima on 6th August, the Russian declaration of war on 8th, and the second bomb on Nagasaki the following day. The Russian attack was of fundamental significance for Japan, for the Soviet Union was the traditional enemy whose invasion of the homeland would inevitably result in the destruction of the Japanese monarchy. The atomic bombs on the other hand were of a different order altogether; they not only raised the spectre of the total obliteration of Japan, but also, and perhaps more importantly, they introduced into warfare an element so different in kind from all that had gone before that the soldier's duty of honour to resist to the death became irrelevant to the situation. This horrendous weapon, 'brighter than a thousand suns' as the Japanese called it, was no corporeal opponent but appeared almost the agent of the deity itself; to bow to this force could imply no dishonour. However, even after the Nagasaki bombing Terauchi, an officer of the old school, was still determined to fight on, and it required a visit from the Imperial House itself, in the person of the Emperor's brother Prince Chichibu, to persuade the Field Marshal to play his part in the general surrender which was about to take

overseas territories still occupied by her armies and that there were grave shortages of food and other essential commodities, while the merchant marine was virtually non-existent and the Imperial navy without a single capital ship. Yet large and efficient land forces still remained both in Japan itself and throughout South East Asia and their morale remained high despite the defeats they had suffered. It appeared likely that Mountbatten's projected invasion would be confronted by the same kind of frenzied bravery in the face of overwhelming odds as had been witnessed in the desperate struggles for Iwo Jima and Okinawa where the Japanese resolution had been astonishing. At Iwo only 216 Japanese were

Left: US troops inspect a smashed Japanese fortificaton and its late occupants on Okinawa. *Above:* The devastation of Hiroshima. The atomic bomb fell approximately one mile from this area. *Below:* Survivors pick their way through the rubble of Nagasaki, on which the second atomic bomb was dropped

Japanese propaganda photo, captioned 'POW in Java relating their fishing adventures' place. It was by such means and by such a narrow margin that the lives of the surviving railway prisoners were preserved.

The surrender was followed by a rapid and hurriedly organised relief operation for the prisoners of war in Siam whose plight was now well known. Harrowing accounts of their treatment by the Japanese had been told by survivors from ships torpedoed on the way to Japan, while information had also been coming in from Group 'E', an organisation which had been set up in early 1944, and whose function was, among other things, to obtain information about the location of POW camps. This had become particularly important after the bombing forces began to extend their raids deep into Siam later in the year. In February 1945 Admiral Mountbatten had been instructed to start firm planning for the recovery of Allied prisoners of war and internees (RAPWI) and a control staff was set up within Allied Land Forces South East Asia for this purpose, to which a Red Cross Co-ordinating Committee and Australian and Indian reception groups for their own prisoners, were affiliated. The trouble was that despite this early planning, the final problem of dealing with the prisoners took the RAPWI organisation rather by surprise, since they had been working on the assumption that they would be recovering prisoners and internees over an extended period as operations progressed, whereas the task which faced them at the Japanese surrender was one of recovering them all simultaneously from camps spread over a vast area. It was estimated that there were about 70,000 prisoners of war in the original South East Asia theatre and a further 55,000 in Java, and they were all dispersed among more than 225 known camps. The whole problem was one of immense urgency since it was known that many prisoners were still suffering and dying from starvation and neglect despite the rather spurious freedom which the Japanese

surrender had given them. The first requirements of the RAPWI organisation was, therefore, to contact the POWs and provide them with food and medical aid, after which those in Siam were to be transported to a collection centre in Rangoon and from there to their homelands.

The rescue operation itself was conducted in two phases, the first, known as 'Operation Birdcage' was mainly concerned with dropping leaflets by air to all known camps, giving notice of the surrender to the Japanese guards, the prisoners and local civilians, followed an hour later by a second flood of leaflets instructing the prisoners to stay in their camps so that food and medical supplies could be dropped to them. The second phase, 'Operation Mastiff', involved the dropping of medical supplies and food, and the parachuting of Red Cross relief teams into the known camps. At the same time parties from Group 'E' and officers from the clandestine organisation known as Force 136, both operating secretly in the occupied territories, were to try to reach the camps. Both groups were then to co-ordinate the dropping of further supplies, making their demands by wireless. The inevitable delay in the signing of the preliminary surrender document by the Japanese delegates in Rangoon meant, however, that 'Birdcage' and 'Mastiff' could not officially start until this ceremony had taken place, but once the operation began it very rapidly brought relief to the prisoners in Siam, who had at least the advantage over their fellows in Malaya, Java and elsewhere, of being in an area which was not directly administered by the Japanese, but by a government which was now very much on the Allies' side and, in addition, much nearer to the British base in Rangoon.

In the prison camps at Pratchai the news of the surrender came while

One of the leaflets dropped during 'Operation Birdcage'

TO ALL ALLIED PRISONERS OF WAR

THE JAPANESE FORCES HAVE SURRENDERED UNCONDITIONALLY AND THE WAR IS OVER

WE will get supplies to you as soon as it is humanly possible and we will make arrangements to get you out. Because of the distances involved it may be some time before we can achieve this.

YOU will help us and yourselves if you act as follows:

1. Stay in your camp until you get further orders from us.

2. Start preparing nominal rolls of personnel giving the fullest particulars.

3. List your most urgent necessities.

4. If you have been starved and underfed for long periods do not eat large quantities of solid food, fruit or vegetables at first. It is dangerous for you to do so. Small quantities at frequent intervals are much safer and will strengthen you far more quickly.

    For those who are really ill or very weak fluids such as broths and soups, making use of the water in which rice and other foods have been boiled, are much the best.

    Gifts of food from the local population should be cooked. We want to get you back home quickly, safe and sound, and we do not want you to risk getting diarrhoea, dysentery and cholera at this last stage.

5. Local authorities and or Allied officers will take charge of your affairs in a very short time. Be guided by their advice.

SPE/1

rumours of the impending massacre of all the POWs were still flourishing, and it was heralded by a parade of the Japanese troops all kitted out in their best uniforms. Somewhat remarkably these fighting units took the Imperial decision without the slightest observable hint of ill-discipline, though when the Japanese commander passed on the news of their freedom to the prisoners' CO, the senior medical officer, he specifically requested a holding over of the celebrations until the fighting units had moved off. At the officers' camp at Nakhon Nayok the announcement came in a less direct manner. The Japanese commander, Captain Neguchi, a notoriously cruel officer, had travelled to Bangkok on 15th August

The surrender of Burma to the Allies:
the Rangoon ceremony, 13th September
1945

held for many months. Stocks of Red Cross parcels were also given out before Neguchi finally admitted, on the afternoon of 17th, that the war was over and that the prisoners were in charge of their own camp. At Kanchanaburi where large numbers of officers still remained, waiting their turn to make the journey to Nakhon Nayok, the surrender announcement came promptly on 16th, though in this case, since the camp lay alongside an important Thai town, it was preceded by rumours from the local people. In most cases the prisoners did not have long to wait before they were contacted by Force 136 and 'E' Group parties or their equivalents from American OSS units, and within a few days most had begun the first stage of the journey home after three and a half long years of captivity.

A total of 4,990 prisoners were recovered from camps in the Saigon area where they had been waiting for months for a ship to take them to Japan, while a further 29,000 were contacted by rescue parties in eleven different camps in Siam. There were also about 6,000 of the survivors of 'F' and 'H' Forces among the 36,000 prisoners of war released in Singapore, and many more of the original railway force with the thousands who were recovered from the labour camps in Japan in the early days of September. Of the total labour force of 61,000 Allied prisoners of war who worked on the Burma-Siam railway 12,399 did not survive the ordeal, and as late as 1956 a special registration unit of the Commonwealth War Graves Commission was still finding graves along the 'railway of death'. Even more tragic were the statistics for the native coolie forces whom the Japanese had employed in much larger numbers. An estimated 270,000 Asians had been impressed to help with the railway work, but of this vast number only some 30,000 were ever traced and

and had obviously received the surrender instructions there, for on his return to the camp he was a changed man, apparently intent on improving his standing with the prisoners before he gave them the official news. On 16th there was an immediate relaxation of restrictions and the following day he handed over to the prisoners thousands of letters which had been with-

repatriated after the surrender. Many of those who were recruited from Burma and Siam may well have got back to their homelands by their own efforts before the war ended, but as many more are likely to have died before they had the chance. It may be that the death toll was as high as 90,000. These figures were horrifying enough in themselves, but the loss of so many young men was also a considerable social problem for the already war-scarred countries from which they came. Malaya for example had supplied 60,000 Tamil coolies for the railway, one tenth of its total Indian population; significantly the Indian community was the only group in multi-racial Malaya still showing a net drop in population in the 1947 census which also grimly indicated that women now represented nearly seventy per cent of the total Tamil community. In an effort to alleviate

the hardship and suffering of the thousands of widows and orphans the Union government distributed a grant of $1,500,000. As always in war, the innocent and the helpless were among the worst sufferers.

In attempting to evaluate and explain the Japanese conduct while constructing this notorious railway one must first of all realise the great difference between the death of these thousands in Burma and Siam, and the massacre of much larger numbers by the Germans in Europe's gas chambers, for example, or by the Japanese in similar deliberate attempts at extermination which took place in several parts of their Pacific Empire. These latter unfortunates were killed as a specific act of policy, they had no choice in the matter and evasion of their fate was impossible; the railway deaths on the other hand were essentially incidental to

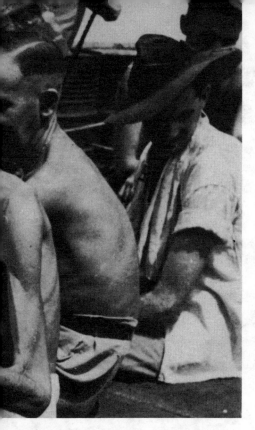

framework of unit organisation and military discipline which managed to withstand the worst shocks which the Japanese could inflict upon it. This meant that the struggle was never purely a personal one and that within limits, everyone was working for the well-being of everyone else. Within such an organisation strict hygiene measures could be observed which, though they meant increased hardship for some, particularly the dysentery sufferers, nevertheless worked for the good of all. Men who were prisoners on the railway have since remarked that those groups which managed to preserve their pre-capitulation unit organisation seemed to fare better than those composed of a heterogeneous mixture of regiments and corps which did not initially cohere and whose framework of social and military organisation was therefore rudimentary. It was the social cohesion of the labour groups that enabled one of the greatest psychological dangers threatening them to be combatted; this was the feeling that imprisonment was a complete break with their past and totally unconnected with their future lives.

The function of keeping alive a sense of continuity in the men was enormously helped by two things: wireless sets and recreational activities. In so remote an area, with the nearest Allied forces hundreds of miles away, reliable news was almost impossible to come by and only the vaguest outline of the main events of the war could be guessed at from reading between the lines of the Japanese propaganda newspapers. It was to the secretly operated radios that all had to turn for any 'hard' news of progress in the war and indeed for any information at all about the 'real' world. As one prisoner later put it, 'Those who survived the years of bondage as prisoners of war in the Far East, will never be able to repay the debt of gratitude which they owe to

the central purpose of getting the strategic line built and operating as quickly as possible. For the prisoners journeying up to Ban Pong or Thanbyuzayat death was therefore by no means inevitable, but life itself was to be a struggle, something that had continually to be fought for. The strain of merely attempting to live was therefore an ever present and almost intolerable burden in all but the easiest of the camps; the remarkable thing is that so few prisoners at the end were suffering from mental illness or had resorted to such desperate means as self-mutilation in order to get evacuated from the worst of the jungle camps. What is equally certain, however is that many men died because they lost the will to carry on the struggle to survive, rather than because they were struck down by a lethal disease.

One vital factor in survival was the

the few who devoted themselves to the job of providing news.' The Japanese tended to believe, or at least pretended to, that a radio set was a transmitter as well as a receiver, and consequently to be caught in possession of one could be fatal. Nevertheless 'canaries', as they were called, were always singing on one stretch of the railway or another, doing more for morale than perhaps anything else during the long captivity. Though their operation was extremely dangerous, the prisoners were helped by the limited knowledge and intelligence of some of their guards. In one camp the commander's own looted radiogram was robbed of parts to provide spares for the prisoners' radio, while in another, lorry batteries were taken

into a hut at night, ostensibly to keep them dry, but for the real purpose of keeping the radio running. The parts of one set did the journey from one camp to another inside the leg bandages of a stretcher patient, while on another occasion the set was hidden among the camp commander's own baggage. One of the first requests that the officers at Nakhon Nayok made to their Japanese commandant Neguchi, after the surrender, was for fresh batteries for the radio which had been working in the camp he ran all the time the railway was being built. The news that filtered into the camps via the radio was sometimes the only asset the doctors had in the

Chungkai camp orchestra's percussion set

A concert party performance at the Chungkai theatre

long up-hill struggle to bring worn out men from the shadow of the grave. Despite the effort and risk involved the benefits from this contact with the world at large were incalculable.

Recreational facilities fulfilled the same kind of function, taking the prisoners out of their immediate environment, giving them other things to think about besides their present plight, and preserving some kind of contact with the civilised world from which they had been torn. During the worst of the 'speedo' period, of course, recreation was quite superfluous, work and sleep consuming all the available hours of the day, but this phase of intense activity was relatively short and there were long months after it when the men had only a limited amount of work to do, insufficient food, and too much time in which to think about their plight. To fill in the long hours all manner of activities were organised; the few dog-eared books which had been preserved were collected and passed around the camps, prisoners gave talks about their civilian occupations. educational classes of

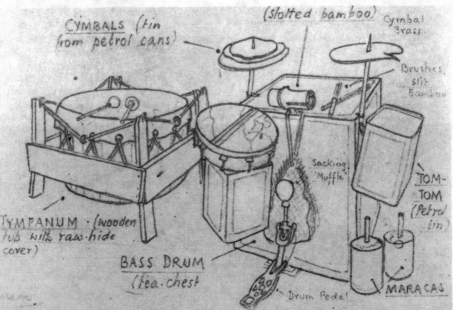

CYMBALS (tin from petrol cans)

(Slotted bamboo)

Cymbal Brass.

Brushes, slit Bamboo

Sacking Muffle

TOM-TOM (Petrol tin)

TYMPANUM - (wooden tub with raw-hide cover)

BASS DRUM (tea-chest

Drum Pedal

MARACAS

The dedication of the Tamarkan
Memorial to those who lost their lives
building the Burma-Siam Railway

all kinds were arranged, some aspiring, by virtue of the qualifications of their organisers and the range of subjects studied, to the title of 'jungle universities'. Concert parties and theatres were also formed, commendable feats of improvisation producing elaborate stage sets and costumes out of jungle raw materials and the few possessions which the men still retained. Evening sing-songs were a feature of many camps, and the base camp at Chungkai eventually boasted an orchestra composed of a scratch lot of instruments varying from a cavalry trumpet to a double bass manufactured from an old packing case. Just as the surgeons in the camp hospitals were working wonders with the crudest of instruments, the talented musicians among their fellows gave concerts of high quality which were almost as valuable, filling in the hours between darkness and bedtime that might otherwise have been spent in introspection in a darkened hut. The Japanese not only permitted but occasionally even encouraged these recreational activities which did so much to maintain sanity and morale.

The final question that needs to be asked about the notorious 'Death Railway' is why, if Japan had freely signed the Hague Convention of 1907 on the law and customs of war, and agreed to observe the terms of the much more detailed Geneva Convention of 1929 on the treatment of prisoners of war, did her treatment of the prisoners who worked on the railway fall so far short of the standards which she had independently chosen to observe? The basic explanation lies in the martial philosophy of the Japanese armed forces which upheld the idea of death in battle as the only alternative to victory. This customary belief was also accepted by Japanese society at large, for when a soldier left his home to join a combatant unit his departure often led to a family ceremony not unlike a funeral rite, in which a lock of hair or a piece of fingernail was kept by the relatives of the departed warrior. From that moment the man was dead so far as his family was concerned, he could only come back alive as a conqueror. The military regulations promulgated by the Ministry of War in January 1942 explicitly stated that every man must die if he could not carry out the task assigned to him. Throughout the Pacific theatre hundreds of thousands of Japanese carried out this order to the letter. Even among the comparatively few Japanese prisoners who were captured many refused to have their names forwarded to Tokyo, and after the general surrender in 1945 refused to return to their families in order to avoid dishonour. Clearly this approach deprived the international conventions of their relevance so far as the Japanese military were concerned, for if their military philosophy denied the possibility of their men being taken prisoner, the conventions were robbed of the principles of reciprocity and mutual benefit which lie at the foundation of all meaningful international agreements. As it turned out, the number of Japanese prisoners in Allied hands had only reached 6,400 by October 1944 as against the 103,000 Allied prisoners held by the Japanese. Moreover, this general attitude to surrender prevented the Japanese military authorities from seeing their prisoners of war as other than dishonoured men whose lives were worthless. Even those among the Japanese military who admitted some knowledge of international law and the conventions took the view that a signature to the Hague Convention by Japan was binding only on the government and not on the army. In these circumstances a lack of consideration for the needs of the railway prisoners beyond such as would enable the line to be built was inevitable.

If this approach made certain that the prisoners' life would be unpleasant, other factors were responsible for the worst of their sufferings. The Hague

Convention laid down that in general, prisoners of war should be accorded the same treatment and enjoy the same living conditions as those of the forces who captured them. Even if the Japanese had obeyed the provisions of the convention, which they did not, this clause would necessarily have subjected their prisoners to methods of discipline and punishment that were almost mediaeval in their brutality, to a medical system that was practically non-existent and to general living conditions that would have been totally unacceptable in any other army. Beatings of Japanese soldiers, including officers, were common, and torture was an accepted part of the order. Even after the capitulation when the Japanese units in Siam were working under the orders of 7th Indian Division, one British brigade commander, himself a hard taskmaster, was shocked to learn that a junior Japanese officer who had failed to carry out an appointed task, was sentenced by his own lieutenant-general to a month's imprisonment with 'bodily torture'. Similar brutalities were therefore inevitably inflicted on the men working on the railway.

In the opinion of one prisoner on the Khwae the Japanese reinforcements who passed alongside the incomplete railway on their way to the Burma front looked as exhausted as, and were driven even harder than the prisoners themselves. Several also reported their amazement at the Japanese treatment of their own wounded, truck-loads of whom were left in appalling conditions, quite without attention of any kind. Some prisoners, despite being more inured to suffering than the ordinary citizen, were even moved to give food and water to these wounded who were ignored by their own compatriots. One badly injured Japanese officer confessed that this was the first time that he had received sustenance of any kind except by his own exertions, during the ninety-eight days of his evacuation from Burma. The Japanese tended to regard sickness in general as shameful, and to maltreat the sick in the belief that this would discourage them from falling ill. Colonel Nakamura, Commander of POW Camps Thailand, explained this attitude succinctly, if in rather fractured English: 'Health follows will . . . Those who fail in charge by lack of health is regarded as most shameful dead.' But the Japanese military system was not solely responsible for the suffering of the railway workers, for in addition they had the debilitating climate and the disease-infested jungle to contend with.

All in all, the unique combination of circumstances produced by the Pacific War flung together thousands of prisoners of war from a civilisation which prized human life and valued high material standards of living and put them under the control of a nation which traditionally emphasised human obligations at the expense of individual rights and extolled triumphs of the spirit over material factors. Ultimately, the forces of western civilisation were triumphant, but not before the Japanese of Southern Army had proved the victory of the will over material problems in building the Burma-Siam railway. A large part of the railway has now been dismantled, the jungle quickly reclaiming the land which was torn from it at such expense and only small sections at each end continue to carry traffic. Yet the story of the building of the line remains a monument to that period of blind inhumanity in Japanese history when a single-minded and ruthless military régime pursued impossible goals at whatever cost in human life. The railway could well serve as the supreme monument to futility: it cost the lives of approximately 393 men, forty-seven of them official prisoners of war and 346 of them Asian 'friends' of Japan, for every mile of its useless track.

Bibliography

Railroad of Death by J Coast (The Commodore Press, London)

The Brave Japanese by K Harrison (Angus & Robertson, London; Tri-Ocean, San Francisco)

The War Against Japan by S W Kirby (HMSO, London)

Kura by C Lumiere (The Jacaranda Press, Melbourne; Tri-Ocean, San Francisco)

Prisoners of War by W W Mason (War History Branch, Department of Internal Affairs, Wellington, New Zealand)

Into the Smother by R Parkin (The Hogarth Press, London; Verry, Lawrence Inc, Mystic, Connecticut)

Bamboo Doctor by S S Pavillard (Macmillan, London)

Prisoner on the Kwai by B Peacock (Blackwood, London)

The Knights of Bushido by Lord Russell of Liverpool (Cassells, London; Dutton, New York)